REREADING LITERATURE
Geoffrey Chaucer

Geoffrey Chaucer

Stephen Knight

Basil Blackwell

© Stephen Knight 1986

First published 1986

Basil Blackwell Ltd
108 Cowley Road, Oxford OX4 1JF, UK

Basil Blackwell Inc.
432 Park Avenue South, Suite 1503,
New York, NY 10012, USA

British Library Cataloguing in Publication data

Knight, Stephen, 1940—
    Geoffrey Chaucer.—(Rereading literature)
    1. Chaucer, Geoffrey—Criticism and interpretation
    I. Title   II. Series
    821'.1   PR 1924

    ISBN 0–631–13881–1
    ISBN 0–631–13882–X Pbk

Library of Congress Cataloging in Publication data

Knight, Stephen Thomas.
    Geoffrey Chaucer.
    (Rereading literature)
    Bibliography: p.
    Includes index.
    1. Chaucer, Geoffrey, d. 1400—Criticism and
interpretation.   I. Title.   II. Series: Re-reading
literature
PR1924.K57   1986   821'.1   85–28775
ISBN 0–631–13881–1

Typeset by Cambrian Typesetters, Frimley, Surrey
Printed in Great Britain by Whitstable Litho Ltd, Whitstable, Kent

For David

Contents

Editor's Preface

It is always convenient for literary criticism to include within its canon an historically remote figure of major importance. For such inclusion helps to collapse the centuries between the writer in question and ourselves, sustaining the myth of an unchanging human nature instantly apprehensible across the purely apparent divide of historical difference. Literature, in this view, is the supreme expression of such stable continuities, all the way from John of Gaunt to Charles de Gaulle; in reflecting back to us a past essentially at one with the present, alien perhaps in thought but more or less identical in feeling, it serves to assure us that the future, too, will be simply more of the same old story. When this particular myth is interwoven with a conservative nostalgia for an 'age of faith', for the comforting assurances of a divinely sanctioned social order, we may be sure that even the most apparently innocent scrutiny of the words on the page is an ideological construct in the final service of political power.

To these particular fictions, the conventional critical processing of Geoffrey Chaucer has frequently added a third, strongly chauvinist dimension. For what after all could be more quintessentially British than the earthy humour, ironic tolerance and genial empiricism of a Chaucer, in contrast to the turgid absolutism of Germany or the arid rationalism of France? Wry, roguish and acceptably bawdy, Chaucer comes to sound in this interpretative account more and more like one's favourite pub landlord. A sane, middling sort of chap, in short, refreshingly free of grim-lipped hectoring or false heroics, eschewing extremes in the name of that well-nigh biological common humanity which undercuts whatever superficial ideological differences may divide us.

One of the achievements of Stephen Knight's study is to challenge such sentimental humanism by offering us a Chaucer firmly rooted in his historical context. *The Book of Fame* presents a searching critique of the culture of the nobility, one made possible in part by Chaucer's peculiarly ambivalent social position between the world of the aristocracy and the emergent forces of the marketplace. *The Parliament of Fowls* interrogates the aristocratic and literary traditions of love, while *Troilus and Criseyde* is shot through in its very forms by an unresolvable tension between an absolute public realm and the powerful inwardness of that private sphere which Criseyde above all symbolises. In the final part of the book, Knight presents a finely detailed poetic sociology of *The Canterbury Tales*, showing once more how Chaucer's poetic forms and political ideology struggle to contain certain turbulent social materials which threaten to transgress them. This fine blending of textual analysis and historical awareness is the hallmark of a book which, as Brecht recommended but T. S. Eliot failed to practise, is able to take the measure of the difference and pastness of the past in a language which reveals, nevertheless, its relevance to our own conditions.

Terry Eagleton

Acknowledgements

I am grateful to the University of Sydney for a period of leave and to the University of Kent and Darwin College for their hospitality while this book was being written. For their varied contributions I should like to thank Peter Brown, Lindy Davidson, David Ellis, Judy Faulkner, Lyn Innes, Ian Jack, John Pryor, Barbara Riddell, Leslie Rogers, Margaret Singer, Alan Ward, John Ward and Michael Wilding. The University of Sydney's Fisher Library has, as usual, been of great assistance and so were staff at the University of Kent's library.

Special thanks are due to Terry Eagleton for the invitation to write this book and for his general guidance and also to Philip Carpenter at Blackwell. As ever, Margaret Knight has been a partner in this activity and so, in her way, has Elizabeth Bronwen.

Introduction

Re-reading Chaucer has been in process for some six hundred years; his work has been constantly re-interpreted and re-valued as changing periods and societies have constructed their own cultural networks of values, interpretations, attitudes and self-defences.

Chaucer's near-contemporaries admired the technical dexterity and wide scope of his poetry, because an author was then seen as a socially responsible craftsman ('maker' is the Middle English for poet), but when writers came to be conceived of as sophisticated renaissance individuals, Chaucer was only seen as a surprisingly learned precursor.[1] Later, among the constrained self-concepts associated with the emergent bourgeois state, readers found an almost noble savagery in Chaucer, ranging in its direction from the vulgarity relished by Dryden and Pope to Coleridge's 'manly cheerfulness'. Some nineteenth century ideologues heard in him a patriotic voice from 'Merry Old England'; a less reductive re-reading linked with the mainline sociocultural tradition of the novel and when Kittredge disseminated the model of Chaucer as a wisely passive observer of humankind, he only brought to a head a dominant attitude of his period. That is still the most widespread reception of the texts, but the special social world of the academy has generated some new and even more conservative versions. The 'new criticism' found Chaucer a master poetic ironist, making wit and euphony a sufficient response to the world. An even more potent ivory tower was constructed by the allegorical school, who deployed their quasi-monastic learning to find in the texts consistent reference to sin and salvation.[2]

All of those and many other re-readings of Chaucer are replete with sociohistorical meaning and function. But it is only recently that a fully social and historical treatment of the texts has been developed, in a period when the old apparent verities of literary criticism have come under widespread attack.

One sustained critique has exposed the traditional canon of 'literature' and the traditional methods of literary criticism as being themselves complicit with and productive of a passive conservative culture. The inherent relations between cultural constructs and their dynamic societies have been steadily laid bare by a number of authors.[3] They offer the theory and some examples of the sociohistorical method: this book is a practical exploration of Chaucer's major work in that way.

There has been a historical Chaucer, of a kind, before now. As English studies rose to respectability and sought weighty self-validating work, Chaucer was, like other writers, treated in a way that claimed to be historical. But it was more a matter of occasions and individuals, restricted to issues such as whose marriage was being symbolized in *The Parliament of Fowls*, did Chaucer actually know people like those in the general prologue to *The Canterbury Tales*? In recent years, though, that reductive trend has been reversed and some light from the world of social and political conflict has been cast on Chaucer's texts.[4]

The type of re-reading that has been foreshadowed so far in this introduction does not fulfil all the possibilities of recent criticism, especially not aspects of what is called 'post-modernist' criticism. In spite of some negative aspects of post-modernism, great advances have been made into the relations between a text (or, better, its textuality) and its social world; into the formal meaning of texts, including previously vexed matters like genre; into the very construction of the notional human subject through the medium of language itself.

It might seem self-limiting to say that this particular re-reading of Chaucer does not deal in any extended way with the strategies and tactics of post-modernism. This limitation rises not from any revulsion from those methods, though at times they can become as self-assertive and reductive as any ironic individualist or awestruck allegorist. Nor, I hope, because of any particular incapacity in the writer of this book. The fact that I have concentrated on the sociohistorical sphere in my deconstruction (or, better, reconstruction) of the special constructs that are

Chaucer's literary texts arises from two particular reasons.

Firstly, there must be a question whether the principle drives of post-modernist criticism are appropriate to a medieval text. As will frequently be argued in the following pages, subjectivity emerges in Chaucer's work, and his texts are rich in semiotic patterns of various kinds. But there are major theoretical and historical problems to be resolved before applying post-modernist methodologies to Chaucer's work in any extended way. The subject in his work is an evanescent and radical creation, not the confident ideological cornerstone of polite and profitable society, as it became in later culture. So the whole positioning of a subject-oriented critique would have to be reversed, accepting as a basic terrain the cultural construction of objectivity, into which the possibility of the subject emerges as a revolutionary force — much as the early formations of bourgeois capitalism had some positive and liberating characteratics.

In an intimately related way, a medieval semiotics would have to attack not the notion of a reified and personaly appropriated domain of language and meaning, but an equally ideological and culturally produced regime of quasi-objective language. Medieval post-modernism, that is, would have to start in another place and work in another direction, with some different tools. While that is a project of absorbing interest and distinct viability, and while its lineaments are becoming discernible,[5] it has not seemed possible to undertake such a preliminary and perhaps provisional project in this book.

Especially so, because the second major reason for creating a socio-historical re-reading is that a thorough study of Chaucer's major works in terms of its relation to the dynamic historical forces of its own period docs not exist and is long overdue. It should have several aspects of value: as a corrective to decades of unhistorical or reductively historical Chaucer criticism; as a means of understanding the mechanisms of production and reception of these potent literary texts; as important evidence towards the general relationship of literature and its social matrix; even as a basis for some further study of Chaucer in terms of the full range of suitably modified modernist critical techniques.

The value and the interest of this study have not been hard to find. Once Chaucer's work is read in a consciously sociohistorical light, it is remarkable how much becomes clear, how differently some things look, how much more powerful and admirable becomes the creative effort of the work itself. Chapter 3 will deal at some length with the implications of the fact, apparently almost unknown to Chaucer scholars, that the Peasants' Revolt of 1381 had Canterbury as a major centre, and that the well-organized peasants marched from there to London, taking a route to be reversed in *The Canterbury Tales*. A related and more immediately developed example comes from *The Book of Fame* (a title to be justified in Chapter 1). The dreamer becomes dissatisfied with the working of the system of honour as it is realized in the House of Fame itself, and he wanders off, vaguely aware of this dissatisfaction and feeling that he should 'wot myself best how y stonde' (one of the moments of radical proto-individualism). He walks down from Fame's castle and sees a very strange thing, which has been usually called the House of Rumour.

Made of wicker, sixty miles long, constantly spinning in the air, it is full of noise and the activity of a working, marketing, chattering, travelling humanity. Messages are sent from here to Fame's house, composed of truth and lies mixed together. Most critics have treated this phenomenal scene on a fully idealistic level as cultural allegory: here are the raw rumours that are mediated by Fame's authority into knowledge or are lost. That is certainly a level at which the poem operates, but not the deepest: Chapter 1 will argue that the poem also and more potently operates as an exposé of the feudal world which was based on castles for security and on honour for the rationale behind its coercive authority.

The 'House of Rumour' has usually been regarded as quite without a source, though some despairing gestures have been made in the direction of Celtic motifs.[6] This is a classic case of historical myopia. Beneath every castle there actually stood the basis of this imaginative creation — the humble, noisy, honour-less and impermanent houses of the villagers who sent their productivity to the castle and augmented its inherently question-able authority. On that specific base Chaucer has projected in an extraordinary piece of analytic symbolism the actual situation of the late fourteenth century in England, when a market economy was developing through the peasant and urban structure that was formerly tied to feudalism, when any serious thinker was aware of a socioeconomic movement contradicting the old order, and when there was a deepening sense that old authorities, such as those based on honour, were facing a crisis. *The Book of Fame*, seen in a sociohistorical way, is not a bungled or overambitious poetic exercise, as most critics have thought, still less a poem about poetry, as is now a fashionable and escapist idea; it is a potent and searching analysis of the world so well known and so powerfully realized by Chaucer.

That is the type of analysis offered in this particular re-reading of Chaucer; for reasons of space it has been necessary to restrict discussion to the three major areas of the dream poems, *Troilus and Criseyde* and *The Canterbury Tales*. In the case of the *Tales*, some have been dealt with less fully than others, not because they are held to be less inherently interesting or less 'good' in some notional scale of eternal values, but because their treatment of contemporary issues has been relatively uncomplicated and without the types of complex condensation and projection found elsewhere, in tales which are subtle and insightful in their socio-historical connections and which, for that reason, have a dynamic character that has in most cases made them extremely interesting to critics whose approach has been only literary. But it is important to note the positions taken and the points made through the less complex tales, because the poem as a whole is a continuing and tense engagement with its period: to concentrate only on the most dynamic tales would falsify the impact of the whole extraordinary text.

If this book can persuade some of its readers to re-read Chaucer's work in the light of the extensive history and socioeconomic work that has been produced on a period where England was both undergoing extraordinarily rapid and dynamic change and from which records survive in numbers that are the envy of continental scholars, then it will have fulfilled its purpose. To see the true impact of the literature, the work involved is more than literary. It involves activities like reading the Paston letters to grasp the structure of family feeling, the *Anonimalle Chronicle* to see what events seemed like from a contemporary viewpoint, a reliable narrative history to know what else was going on; it is also important to have a grasp of a sound economic treatment of the period and to read the biographies of major figures to pick up connections between people, events and places that may lie within the literary texts.[7]

The reward for this sort of work is double. The texts themselves spring into dynamic and conflicted life, potent realizers of the conflicts of the period as they appeared to one of the most imaginatively receptive and analytically rigorous minds of the time. But that thorough knowledge of texts from another period casts a penetrating light on the present. A process of interwoven continuity and contrast exposes the social role of culture in our own period, whether the formations of the medieval text have a surprising continuity or a startling contrast with modern practices and attitudes — both demand an explanation of the underlying sociohistorical formations.

To re-read the Chaucerian texts in terms of their social and historical meaning and function is to be constantly aware of the political role of all culture in all periods — a re-reading of Chaucer that can produce socio-historical interpretations of the texts' receptions through time and is particularly relevant to the present state of society and its culture.

1 Dream Poems and Chaucer's World

I Preface

Chaucer is remembered as a writer of narratives, both noble and vulgar. But it was through non-narrative dream poems that he established himself, and it is through them that his poetry and his historical imagination are best approached.

The young Chaucer would have identified the narrative mode with the relatively simple English romances; he had not yet encountered the complex medieval Italian stories, and though he knew French well, the sophisticated romances of earlier centuries had been displaced in French aristocratic circles by dream allegories about love. Since Chaucer was a court official with aspirations to be a serious poet, the French dream poems provided the obvious path for him to follow in English.

But the form had wider possibilities. The dream itself was a basic mode for medieval analysis of society. Dreams were taken seriously as ways of revealing a truth that the waking individual could not attain.[1] Two important late classical sources for Chaucer were dreams (Boethius's *Consolation of Philosophy* and Macrobius's version of the *Dream of Scipio*) and so were three medieval works of high subtlety, enormous range and biting social analysis, the *Roman de la Rose* and *The Divine Comedy* (both of which were used by Chaucer) and *Piers Plowman*, a contemporary English work that matches his own perception of late fourteenth century social forces. When he adopted the dream mode Chaucer was not only using a form appropriate to a leisured aristocracy: he was enabling himself to adventure into the highest ranges of medieval art and social analysis.

Three dream poems are central in Chaucer's work, *The Book of the Duchess*, *The Book of Fame* (that title will be explained later) and *The Parliament of Fowls*. Chaucer worked on other dream poems: he translated part of the *Roman de la Rose*, the later *Legend of Good Women* has a dream prologue and there are sleeping sequences in several of his other works. But the three major dream poems, which form a coherent group, reveal on a readily comprehensible scale Chaucer's treatment of his surrounding world, and so form a suitable introduction to a book like this, not so much about Chaucer's life and poetry as about the way in which his art realizes imaginatively the historical forces of a particularly dynamic period.

II *The Book of the Duchess*: 'sorwful ymagynacioun'

The surviving records of Chaucer's life fill a plump volume.[2] More is known about him than Shakespeare or most writers before relatively modern times because so much of his life was spent serving the crown in a context where records were carefully kept of appointments, duties and rewards. In the early stage of his career, until 1374, he was first a household official for the Countess of Ulster (wife to Prince Lionel, Edward III's third son); after that he worked directly for the king as a confidential aide and negotiator. He was not born into the aristocracy or even the gentry, but his position developed from the status gained by his wine-merchant father, who was the king's deputy butler in Southampton, a quite important post involving the provisioning of armies leaving for France.

Like some other officials of the aristocracy Chaucer also worked as a poet, both to entertain lords and ladies and, like bards of the past, to provide cultural rationalization of their power. Guillaume Machaut, the French poet who is Chaucer's major early source, wrote poems of great elegance which create the image of a leisured nobility and also insist on royal authority: the king judges the debates on love and courtesy. Two of these poems provide the basis for Chaucer's earliest surviving work of substance, *The Book of the Duchess*. Written for an aristocratic audience, it operates entirely within the noble world, concentrating on its problems and its values.[3]

Its stimulus was the death of Blanche, Duchess of Lancaster. She died of plague in 1368, not 1369 as used to be thought. The poem seems to have been written soon afterwards, 'in youthe' as the Man of Law says in *The Canterbury Tales*.[4] The French-derived style and material, the occasionally clumsy writing (such as repetition in 67–74, awkward rhymes at 309–10, 341–2, 471–2) all suggest this is an early work as, pre-eminently, does its firmly aristocratic ideology.

Blanche had been Duchess of Lancaster in her own right. John of Gaunt, the king's fourth son, was merely a fairly poor Earl when he married her and so became Duke in 1359. The poem speaks at length about 'the faire White', insisting in the name on its English medium. Her beauty, grace and concordant authority are fully realized, but this is far from an elegy: nothing is said about her happiness in heaven, nor is the transience of earthly glory ever mentioned — standard features of Christian remembrance. The poem operates in the present after her death, and its central problem is the impact her passing has on a figure called 'Man in Black'. He is not literally John of Gaunt — Man in Black is beardless and twenty four (455–6): Gaunt was a vigorous twenty eight when Blanche died. Man in Black is a figure of immaturity and too much sorrow, who, because of his reaction to his loss, has become dysfunctional as an aristocrat. The poem celebrates 'White' and remembers her grandly, but crucially it insists that the public, active, aristocratic life must continue. Chaucer writes, that is, for the surviving Duke, with delicacy and tact and with a clear firmness that is authorized by the imaginative power of the poem. That Gaunt recognized its value is suggested by his grant in 1374 of a pension for life to Chaucer 'for the good and agreeable service our friend Geoffrey Chaucer has done us'.[5]

This is a dream poem, not a narrative, and it is written in a fully Gothic mode. That is, it does not steadily work towards a dramatic climax of action and meaning like the novel or the renaissance play: its theme is stated and then made authoritative throughout the work.[6] More like a sermon with a text, it establishes in the opening lines the theme that the poem will amplify and justify. The narrator firstly states that he is distraught through his constant obsession with grief:

> . . . sorwful ymagynacioun
> Ys alway hooly in my mynde.

(14–15)

And then just as briskly and clearly he asserts the common knowledge that this is an unnatural and ultimately fatal attitude:

> And wel ye woot, agaynes kynde
> Hyt were to lyven in thys wyse;
> For nature wolde nat suffyse
> To noon erthly creature
> Nat longe tyme to endure
> Withoute slep and be in sorwe.

(16–21)

That is not the narrator's own insightful analysis. Like the aristocratic courtier, the medieval poet has no personal status or individual authority: the truth he relates is known to all — 'wel ye woot' (16) — and is a matter of widely observed and natural forces. In the same impersonal way, what the cause of the narrator's sorrow might be is not of any relevance. Lines 30–43 state this firmly, but that has not stopped modern scholars speculating about the biographic details behind the passage.[7] This narrator is a functionary of the poem, setting up certain truths at the beginning, and later initiating their fuller realization. The narrator's role has blurred the poem for many critics for whom modern individualism obscures the actual mode of the medieval text, but that approach has been firmly corrected by recent scholars.[8]

Having stated from general experience the fatal nature of too much sorrow, the narrator turns to that other source of knowledge in the medieval world, 'auctoritee', the equally non-individual wisdom found in literature and scholarship. Unable to sleep, he reads a book handed to him (in fully feudal fashion) by 'oon' (47), some nameless, unconsidered servant. It must be Ovid's *Metamorphoses*, because the story is that of 'Seys and Alcyone'. King Ceyx died suddenly and Queen Alcione sorrowed bitterly. Juno sent the dead king to her in a dream, to insist on the need to accept the fact of his death. Nevertheless, Alcione died from her unrelieved sorrow, but through the pity of the gods King and Queen were given a new life together in the form of birds.

Chaucer, as usual, tells the story in his own way, for his own purposes.[9] He stresses the human feeling of 'Alcyone' and omits the happy ending. Here she simply dies, to provide dramatic and learned authorization of the narrator's opening remarks. Chaucer also adds comedy and colour to the sequence, especially in the droll presentation of sleep-drugged Morpheus. Like many of the Chaucer's comic treatments and ironic asides, this has bothered scholars who follow the post-medieval concept of unity of tone in literature – a concept, of course, quite flexible in artists like Shakespeare and Dickens who were as aware as Chaucer of the power of comedy both to relieve and intensify a serious response, especially in an orally performed medium. Such tonal variety was a basic practice in all Gothic art, whether it was a secular poem or an illustrated collection of psalms.

The narrator decides to give Morpheus, god of sleep, the present of a bed and as a result he himself is given sleep. This too has been found comic. So it is, as a relieving interlude: but it is also, as non-historical criticism has not realized, a fully feudal reward. Kings and princes who existed in and through the feudal mode of production rewarded people with wine, clothes, tracts of land but not with cash: it was not central to that 'use economy'. Although fourteenth century society was moving rapidly towards a cash-based 'exchange economy', as some of Chaucer's own payments and even his characters indicate, the development was by no means complete and the concept of useful rewards was still dominant in the aristocratic context.

As he dreams, the narrator is at the heart of a functioning feudal court. He has a splendid bedroom with windows that tell a story, like the stained glass in Canterbury Cathedral which recounts in great detail some of the miracles of St Thomas. The stories told here, though, are archetypes of chivalry and courtesy, the legend of Troy and *The Romance of the Rose*. Then the dreamer rides out to join a hunt, that central activity of noble life through which cavalrymen kept themselves and their horses fit for war, demonstrated their courage and skill and also won food from their richly stocked forests (which were carefully protected from lower class access). This hunt is especially noble, led by the 'emperour Octovyen' (368). Better known as Augustus, the ruler of Rome at its most powerful, he symbolizes secular authority; vigorous dynamic poetry realizes the noble world in highly organized and potent life (348–84).

But the poem and its narrator drift away from that busy, honorific scene. He follows a 'whelp' (a hunting dog too immature to run with the pack) and together they go through a forest of great trees and abundant natural life to find a figure equally immature and excluded from that vital and social world.

He is a man in black, sitting alone, hanging his head, intoning words without music about the sorrow that has desocialized him. It is immediately obvious that his state was the object of the narrator's opening remarks and the story of Seys and Alcyone, and the narrator rephrases his well-known truth about sorrow (466–69).

Privacy is so central a value in the modern world that it is important to stress its essential aberrance in medieval society. People were hardly ever alone: they ate, lived, slept and even experienced books in company. The concept of the human being — ontology — was as a social animal; private feelings, whether of love, vengeance or despair, were consistently seen as being, however understandable, a threat to the common social good. It has been established that honour was a prime value, publicly known and publicly asserted; shame, its opposite, was equally a public matter, an absolute exclusion from the honoured society.[10] This crucial structure was not some perverse medieval quirk: when sustenance and security depended on collective effort rather than on technological power, when an economy was not based on wealth privately gathered and laid out for profit, the individual was not the treasured self-concept it has become. There was private effort and feeling in the period, of course, just as there is much collective reality in the modern world, but medieval concepts of being and knowing were essentially public and social: the structure was the precise reverse of the modern position.

The lonely Man in Black is an emblem of aristocratic dysfunction, an unnatural entity who must be resocialized or wither away, like that consistent figure in romance, the knight run wild in the forest, Lancelot, Tristram or Yvain. The narrator, acting as a functionary of the poem's meaning, offers talk and human sympathetic context. The process of resocialization seems possible because Man in Black is not entirely out of touch with his former noble state and its values. He recognises, but rejects, bookish authority as a mode of knowing (568–90). When he says 'Y am sorwe, and sorwe ys y' (597) he used the rhetorical device of *contentio*, turning a phrase or line on its head for emphasis. Such rhetoric was associated with and helped to construct established learning and high social status. The whole following speech is a stylish reversal, asserting the innate nobility which he has lost and which his language implies he may regain; it also states the self-concept of the luxurious noble world in the positive things

that have for him become negative: song, laughtre, glade
thoghtes, ydelnesse, reste, wele, good, pleynge, delyt, hele,
sykernesse, lyght, wyt, day, love, slep, myrthe, meles and
countenaunce – which means face, status and honour (599–613).

The word 'sorwe' dominates this whole sequence, and a basic
way in which the poem operates is through key words – a
common practice in poetry that was designed to be performed
aloud, creating through repeated concepts a pattern of meaning
accessible to the listener. Sorrow was introduced by the narrator,
was found in Ovid's book and recurs through Man in Black's
opening statement, dominating both the introduction (591–7)
and the conclusion (700–09). As the narrator ushers the knight
through his long reminiscence of his lost love, the word and fact of
sorrow disappear (as is pointed out in 1104–7), being largely
replaced, as a repetitive motif, by a benign and shared response
to what was 'swete'. When sorrow recurs it is that of a hopeful
lover (1184, 1250) and, finally, the shared joy and sorrow of a
happy couple (1293).

This verbal process of resocialization meshes with the creation
of a poetic monument to Blanche. Some modern critics have
elaborated psychological aspects of consolation, but they have
essentially misplaced the sphere of action of the poem[11] It does
not 'work through' John of Gaunt's grief in terms of modern and
individualist concepts of the personality. It operates, rather, in
fully medieval form, creating a public realization of the splendour
of Blanche and of Gaunt's relationship with her: so feeling is
liberated from the private and dysfunctional terrain into a fully
socialized present.

Blanche, it is important to see, is not presented as Gaunt's, or
Man in Black's, memory of her; she is not realized in the minute
and individualistic terms of the characters of a novel, but in the
highly conventional collective language of the medieval text. Her
beauty is one of poise, control, measure and stately authority,
transcendent of any private aberration. All that is said about her
is publicly visible and generally acknowledged to be so, like her
flawless noble beauty:

> But swich a fairnesse of a nekke
> Had that swete that boon nor brekke
> Nas ther non sene that myssat.
> Hyt was whit, smothe, streght, and pure flat,

> Withouten hole; or canel-boon,
> As be semynge, had she noon.
> Hyr throte, as I have now memoyre,
> Semed a round tour of yvoyre,
> Of good gretnesse, and noght to gret.
>
> (939–47)

Her pre-eminence itself is seen in a social context, as the crowning glory of a society in action:

> For I dar swere wel, yif that she
> Had among ten thousand be,
> She wolde have be, at the leste,
> A chef myrour of al the feste,
> Thogh they had stonden in a rowe,
> To mennes eyen that koude have knowe.
> For wher-so men had pleyd or waked,
> Me thoghte the felawsshyppe as naked
> Withouten hir, that saugh I oones
> As a corowne withoute stones.
>
> (971–90)

The narrator misses — and so emphasizes — this public social role when he suggests the memory might be single and partial; he is urgently corrected by Man in Black (1049–53), who then goes on to surround this monument to Blanche with literary authorities to strengthen the non-individualist grandeur of her and of their love (1056–74). He continues from first love to equal marriage, through the formal stages of courtly love or *fin amor*, as it was called in the period. This was more than a noble game or a literary fiction, as most scholars present it. Just as chivalry ideologically concealed the 'competitive assertiveness' of rival cavalrymen,[12] so the courtesy of love provided both a general aura of noble behaviour and a specific masking of the real relations between upper-class men and women. The social world was sternly patriarchal and in many instances a woman's own power and wealth were appropriated as well as her personal independence — Blanche herself is a classical example. Courtly romance actually took its origin in a period when newly disinherited younger sons needed to find wealthy unmarried women, either in reality or in the wish-fulfilment of romance.[13]

With the formal and publicly powerful beauty of 'good faire

White' established and the equally formal and ideological pattern of courtly love completed, the poem has erected its effective monument. All the functional narrator needs to do is to prompt Man in Black to state the present reality and offer human sympathy in the language of post-ceremonial normalcy and renewed social function.

'She ys ded!' 'Nay!' 'Yis, be my trouthe!'
'Is that youre los? Be God, hyt ys routhe!'

(1309–10)

At once White, Man in Black and the whole encounter dissipate; their cultural work is done. The hunt, frozen when this sequence of aristocratic dysfunction started, springs into life and 'thys kyng Gan homwardes for to ryde' (1314–15).

In keeping with the realism of Man in Black's final words, the hunt returns to a place of lightly coded historical existence:

A long castel, with walles white,
By seynt Johan! on a ryche hil

(1318–19)

John, Earl of Richmond and Duke of Lancaster, lives here; the imperial hunter Octovyen is now an emblem of renewed aristocratic function, just as the immature Man in Black was an emblem of too much sorrow. The work of reconstructing a whole public persona, healed of private wounds, is done, and the poem can end.

Imaginatively vivid and ideologically simplistic, *The Book of the Duchess* reveals a skilful poet who has not yet probed the structures of his world, but who reproduces brilliantly the dominant culture and ideology of his immediate milieu. His social position was to change and a new environment, economic, cultural and physical, would stimulate a radically different and distinctly radical poem, whose nature and importance has been misunderstood by most Chaucerians.

III   *The Book of Fame*: 'I wot myself best how y stonde'

This poem is usually called 'The House of Fame'; that title is found in some manuscripts, but scribes often named a text from its most notable sequence. The poet, in his Retractions to *The Canterbury Tales* speaks of his 'book of fame' and this, 'Chaucer's final title' as Bennett describes it,[14] is the most suitable for a poem which inquires with a restless intelligence into the nature of fame in a wide-ranging sense of honour as a social force — its essential medieval role (see p. 12). The 'House' of Fame herself is only one of the locations for this searching investigation. It is the place linked with the traditional aristocracy and their values, and the deep scepticism of that sequence, the revelation of honour's flimsy and fortuitous basis, is the most radical single step in the poem, breaking sharply as it does with the contentedly aristocratic ideology of *The Book of the Duchess*.

Chaucer's own career underwent a related shift between the two poems. Partly in reward for his good services as a royal agent, partly to use more profitably his assiduity and literary skills, he was appointed Controller of Customs in June 1374: the arduous 'rekeynynges' that were involved are mentioned in *The Book of Fame* (652–3). It was a curious position, especially in social terms. The Controller swore not only to be faithful and assiduous, as usual in such posts, but also to keep his rolls in his own hand.[15] This was no sinecure for which a permanent deputy could be appointed. The Controller's accounts were a careful check on those kept by the Collector, who actually took the customs dues and passed a proportion on to the king: Chaucer's job was to see the king was not cheated. So he was still a royal operative, but no longer working in the supportive ambience of the court; plunged into the heart of the mercantile world, he had nevertheless to keep fidelity to his old allegiance. It is a striking example of the marginality that is the position of most powerful social analysts, like Charles Dickens, son of a provincial bankrupt, or Karl Marx, a Christianized Jew. Displacement brings clarity of focus upon both the past and the present environment.

The reference to Chaucer's work dates *The Book of Fame* between 1374 and 1385, when he gave up the post after an unusually long tenure.[16] It seems that the poem should be dated early in that period, because although Chaucer shows a growing familiarity with Italian poetry, it is by no means complete. Boccaccio is not an influence on the work, and a mistake about Scipio (916) is corrected in *The Parliament of Fowls* — he was no king, though the *Roman de la Rose* said he was. This developing Italian knowledge is usually associated with the trip made to

Italy for the king in 1372–3[17] but Chaucer would have met many Italians through the customs, merchants and bankers who would not necessarily be uncultured: Boccaccio himself had worked for the banking house of the Bardi.

The essence of *The Book of Fame* is that the French love vision (the whole basis of *The Book of the Duchess*) is here diverted towards that other kind of medieval dream, the serious analysis of the world and its values. The dreamer goes to Venus' temple in Book I and at the opening of Book II he is promised love 'tydynges' (675), but the poem bears down on 'tidynges' as news and fame, the media of information and honour, rather than on the topic of love. Courtly love and aristocratic authority had supported each other in the French love poems and in upper class life, but this poem digs deeply into the foundations of the noble world and its culture and finds them without secure values. Personally repositioned outside the court, thrust into the core of the newly and rapidly developing mercantile world, Chaucer in his art rejects old certainties and probes for a new place to stand. He does so with such determination and scepticism that after establishing the position for a final statement of true validity, when the dreamer has encountered at last 'a man of gret auctoritee' (2158), the poem ends unfinished, unable to realize such security.

As with *The Book of the Duchess*, the plan of the poem is implied in the opening sequence, but here its development takes it away from its promised scheme: this art is radical and dynamic, not static and conservative. Dream poems usually had a sequence which discussed dreams themselves, to assert through learned authority the validity of the mode itself (280–9 in *The Book of the Duchess*). Chaucer's opening sequence in *The Book of Fame* bombards the reader with 'a plethora of contradictory information about dreams'.[18] The effect is bewilderment and the only hope is prayer: the first line, 'God turne us every dreem to good', is repeated at the end of the sequence. That predicts an overall scheme of the poem: a welter of complex and self-destructing material will be laid out before dreamer and audience and then authority will finally be found in a brief but firm statement of heavenly consolation. But this poem will strain its own imagination beyond such a consoling conclusion: it confronts the conflicted historical world too closely and too frankly to permit that comforting withdrawal.

Innovation and conflict are dominant as the poem begins. The narrator's invocation, like the division into books itself, proclaims an artistic ambition in this poem that quite elevates the submerged author of the typical medieval text — and of *The Book of the Duchess*. But in doing so, a strain is revealed: the author is anxious for personal fame and this brings with it a prickly individualism as he curses those who will not like his poem (94–108).

He begins sombrely in December, no time for a benign, springlike love vision. The temple of Venus is the place, but here love is without any smiling aspect. The first book recounts the story of Aeneas, discovered on some dream-like expanding tablet of brass. In *The Book of the Duchess* literature neatly confirmed the narrator's opening statement; so it does here, but all he has provided is a set of gestures towards confusion. Scholars have fretted over this first book, feeling it does not mesh with the others. A critic as perceptive as Muscatine has found the whole poem unsatisfactory, writing it off as something like passages from an author's notes.[19] But if the poem is seen as a whole book ranging over the topic of fame, this first sequence has its place.

Two accounts of Aeneas were known in the middle ages — his fame was itself dual and doubtful. Virgil's *Aeneid* made him the great founder of Rome, escaping from the sack of Troy, enduring hardships and distractions before coming to Italy and founding the city. One of the detours was a love affair with Dido, Queen of Carthage, which ended when his mission drove him on and she committed suicide. Ovid, however, represented Aeneas as Dido's betrayer, as a fickle and selfish lover who destroyed a noble queen. In this dream literary authority itself is not clear and certain.

Delany has written forcefully about the poem's place in the tradition of late medieval scepticism,[20] but the spirit of inquiry goes beyond an unmasking of cultural contradictions. Book I makes it clear that it is not just fame as reputation that is of uncertain value. Fame as a substantive social force, that is as honour, is the actual mechanism of the disaster Chaucer recounts. It is Aeneas' quest for honour, driven on by Venus (not as Goddess of love, but as his own guiding deity — another duality) that takes him from Carthage to Rome, and the poem asserts that fact in affirmative tones (427–32). And it is Dido's lack of good fame, her own social shame as a betrayed woman, that drives her to suicide (345–52). Book I is a powerful and disturbing survey of fame as it is treated in literary authorities and also as it operates on people in society.

The fame and honour that gave status and power in the aristocratic world are found to be both confusing and destructive, and accordingly, as Book I ends, the narrator finds himself in no comfortable and vital social world as he did in *The Book of the Duchess*, but alone, in a desert. The first person pronoun dominates his painful view of his desperately desocialized state:

> When I out at the dores cam
> I faste aboute me beheld.
> Then sawgh I but a large feld,
> As fer as that I myghte see,
> Withouten toun, or hous, or tree,
> Or bush, or grass, or eryd lond;

(480–5)

As when he was faced with contradictory information about dreams, his response to literary enigmas of fame is to pray (492–4) and looking up he sees a splendid eagle. It descends, and then bears him away, up into the sky. Not into the heavens, though. Although the eagle itself is borrowed from Dante's *Divine Comedy*, and although it seems invoked by a prayer, it is not an agent of Christian confidence, however much allegorical critics have strained to make it so.[21] This particular poem makes the eagle bear a quite different value, a type of human knowledge that was in Chaucer's day growing in power and reputation, particularly in England. Chaucer himself wrote one, probably two, books of scientific education (*The Treatise on the Astrolabe* and, it seems, *The Equatory of the Planets*) and his friend Ralph Strode was almost certainly the Oxford mathematician of that name. What in *The Parliament of Fowls* Chaucer will call 'this newe science that men lere' (25) is in Book II offered as a way of approaching the strange phenomenon of fame, both as a medium of knowledge and as a structural force in society.

The eagle is not so much God's messenger as a lecturer in physics. He explains the mechanism of sound as it was then understood and takes the dreamer, as if on a field trip, to the 'House of Fame', where all earthly sounds come together and where the drama of honour and shame is re-enacted. But this project, to decode through human intelligence and imagination what literary authority left in confusion, is a huge and daring venture in a medieval world where the ideology of science as provider of security, mental and physical, was centuries away from development. The poem asserts the fearful bravado of the scheme, and the concomitant isolation of the intellectual adventurer. He is personalized as Geffrey (729) – a very unusual feature in medieval fiction, though one that Dante had already dared – and he is set in the poet's own context, emphasizing the asocial character of his work as Controller (647–51). Then Book II depicts the solitary poet flying high in his inquiries and leaving behind the comforting presence of the physical world (896–909). He cringes from his awe-inspiring adventure; he would prefer to read books, fearing that the vision of this 'newe science' will daunt him – 'y am now to old' (995), and dazzle him – 'Hyt shulde shenden al my syghte' (1016). But the eagle that his determined and privatized intelligence has invoked lands him at Fame's castle, forced to look and listen, to be both dazzled and daunted.

Several things in this second book have worried critics. The eagle has a humorous style, the narrator is presented as foolish, the science itself has seemed a parody. But the lecture is mainstream medieval physics, and while limited from a modern standpoint is not wholly contemptible.[22] The uneven tone and comic touches realize the perilous and potentially confusing nature of the attempt, a deliberate reduction of the narrator to make less disturbing his actually very ambitious project.

Book II was invoked in the self-conscious and so risky context of a single narrator's self and his adventuring brain (523–5); Book III seems to have gained some confidence from Book II, because here Apollo is invoked as the god of 'science and of lyght' (1091). The opening sequence is a lucid critique of the world of aristocratic honour and high culture through the centuries. Fame's house is a castle, perched like so many on a safe hilltop; but neither itself nor its contents are securely based. The ice on which it stands is an untrustworthy foundation and the names carved on it with honour can melt in the sun – except, in an image both literal and deeply suggestive, where the natural light never reaches because of the shadow cast by the establishment of fame. Unnatural, self-defensive, fortuitous – these implications will be followed up.

A set of exotic images suggest the inauthentic character of this world of fame: the castle is built of beryl, beautiful but brittle (1184) and itself with magnifying properties (1290); yet it is also plated with gold, both splendid and impractical and also a sign of seeming wealth unreliably based (1341–6). The castle's gate is shaped with an art that is no more than artifice (1297) and in a similar way, discerning manipulation within an ostensibly impressive structure, the list of poets and musicians who transmit honour turns (most unusually[23]) into a litany of illusionists and magicians (1214–81). Great poets are found in Fame's hall as the mediators of heroic and national glory, but they too are questioned, reduced in simile to rooks, the noisiest and most foolish of sociable birds (1514–16).

The nature of fame has been negatively depicted in description and environment, and it is now seen in action, an experience as confusing and disturbing as any so far in this wintry dream. Groups of petitioners come in one after another and ask for fame of some sort or another — some seek glory, some ask for their names to be forgotten, one group even shamelessly asks for shame itself. The dramatic point, made with vivid impact, is that fame is essentially whimsical. Identical groups receive different results; Fame sometimes conceals shameful deeds, she sometimes publishes good deeds that modest people want kept quiet, and in each case her verdict is irreversible.

This is not only a strongly negative analysis of fame and its mechanisms. It is economically and socially deeply rooted. The scene presents the castle of a powerful noble, who is visited by suitors and who gives or withholds at whim profitable support or socially destructive opposition. The operation of the royal or baronial court, feudal and legal, is the essential structure, and upon that social reality a theoretical analysis is imposed. No contemporary reader would think, as modern critics tend to do in their anti-historical and asocial way, that this poem is about poetry, or is just a fanciful literary exercise. Feudal society and its cultural support system are under searching imaginative attack.

The narrator indicates his dissent from this whole structure when he draws aside and says he has no care for Fame:

> Sufficeth me, as I were ded,
> That no wight have my name in honde.
> I wot myself best how y stonde;
>
> (1876–8)

That is not a positive and confident stance; it is merely a strong sense that ill-founded fame and its social world are not securely based. An essentially Christian moral poem would at this point turn to heavenly certitude. But this text continues to deal, through the mediations of imaginative art, with the late medieval world, not some Christian retirement from it. As if in response to his private dissent, the narrator is taken to another place, usually called the 'House of Rumour'. But that expression is not used in the poem; the strange edifice he sees is certainly filled with rumour and 'tidynges' of all sorts that go to Fame's house and there win her (now dubious) authority or are ignored. But, as has been argued, Fame's house was not just about fame meaning news, but also fame meaning socially powerful honour. The so-called 'House of Rumour' is also a social reality, as has been suggested in the Introduction, pp. 4–5. It represents the world of medieval productivity of peasants and artisans and merchants, with all its contemporary complexity and inherent threat to the feudal world.

The poem inspects this other world in as imaginative, thorough and disturbing a way as it did the hall of fame. The images of motion, size and strangely stable flimsiness (1924–6, 1935–40, 1957, 1980–2) catch the essence of the world outside the castle in Chaucer's time, in which he was now inserted, in life as in this poem. Mobility is a feature constantly remarked in the period (especially in *Piers Plowman*) and it is the essence of the developing market economy, whether at the simple level of observed busy-ness or at the deeper level of Marx's analysis of money circulation and carrying trade. The size of the house is also a contemporary image; the ganglion of London's economic range was just about 'sixty myle of length' (1979) and that was the distance from which peasants marched on London in 1381. The strange place that produces the raw material for the castle is a brilliantly projected image of the non-feudal world that was still subdued by the fame and the power of the world it served, but was increasingly a pullulating commercial marketplace, emerging as a force in its own right and taking, or seizing as it seemed, its own place in history.

The man who was neither merchant nor royal household official could see with dismaying clarity both the old world of feudal power and the new world of the productive market. To him, neither held secure values or any appeal: Fame's house has been dealt with negatively at length; this other place is disorderly and sends lies and truth together to the castle (2088–109). As in Book I, in Book III the poet still realizes an unbridgeable and disturbing duality. The importance of Book III, though, is that this duality is no longer a literary treatment of a past age offering no more than scepticism, but is rather an entirely original and unmatched analysis of social structures and values in the late fourteenth century. The poet's historical imagination has pursued a lonely and chilly quest in the desert of isolation, and has created visions of strange and compelling analytic power, seeing both the whimsical tyranny of aristocratic appropriation, coercion and cultural self-validation and then the turbulent forces typified by the chaotic world of marketplace activities and cultural confusion.

This realization of historical contradiction is so strong, the poet's contact with his own social world is so compulsive, that the final words of great authority cannot be spoken. There is no stable secular authority, as the poem has shown. It also refuses the consoling dislocation of a Christian ending. The poem reveals its own authority in the world of historical forces by refusing to find room for the imposed authority of a world-escaping church. In his later works Chaucer was able to conclude his poems in that way, though they continued to be powerful realizations of the contemporary world — yet never again as disturbing and pungently critical as the unmatched *Book of Fame*.

IV   *The Parliament of Fowls*: 'commune profyt'

The shortest and most compact of the dream poems, *The Parliament of Fowls*, is later than *The Book of Fame*, as its correct treatment of Scipio proves and as is suggested by its wider knowledge of Italian literature. Many commentators have dated it in 1382, but this only rests on a doubtful astrological reference in line 117, as if Chaucer put his head out of the window at that moment. For reasons that will be explained, it seems that the late 1370s is the period of composition

The Parliament of Fowls follows *The Book of Fame* in other ways. It diverts the topic of love into a realization of contemporary conflict, it juxtaposes unsatisfactory literary tradition with actual social disorder, it offers, rather more strongly than before, a Christian response that remains unconfirmed. But where in *The*

Book of Fame art itself seemed brought under suspicion as a mediator of ill-founded honour, in *The Parliament of Fowls* the art of poetry has value through being the agent of ideological resolution — though not without some trace of the strain which finally disrupted *The Book of Fame*. Here the cool, isolated onlooker is less anxious and more able to stand as an artist: an important stage in culture itself is shaped in addition to the potent treatment of contemporary forces, both general and quite specific.

Throughout the late 1370s Chaucer remained at work in the Customs, but also acted on special occasions as a royal emissary. He already knew well members of a loose group of professional men, including scholars, poets, lawyers and higher civil servants, an intelligentsia of the period that has been described recently by several scholars.[24] 'The circle of Chaucer'[25] is a term that may privilege too much the writer's place in the group, but it does suggest that among these men who valued thought, art and analysis the non-feudal, non-mercantile person Chaucer had become was able to find at least some social nexus.

Intellectual the group may have been, but aesthetes they were not; they were serious interpreters of their society, producing apart from Chaucer's work the earnest weight of John Gower or the sober moralism of the Lollard knights, such as Clanvowe's *The Two Ways*.[26] The opening stanzas of *The Parliament of Fowls* state at once the value found in books, but indicate that such authorities fall short of certainty in the world of human experience. The narrator speaks of love in confident and traditional literary aphorisms, but then adopts a quite different and uncertain rhythm in lines 5–6 and the last line of this opening stanza states monosyllabically his transfixed bemusement in the face of actuality:

Nat wot I tell wher that I flete or synke.

(7)

To resolve this doubt and resume his original confidence, he turns to books.

As in each dream poem, literary authority is offered; this time it is Cicero's *Dream of Scipio* as transmitted and expanded by Macrobius who was, like Boethius, one of the late classical and Christian authors that Chaucer evidently valued highly, presumably because they were neither theologically or spiritually excessive, but dealt with the experience of the world in moral and Christian terms. The narrator recounts the essence of this book, without significant distortion and in a notably cool style. In one way that is suitable: Auerbach has explained how 'sermo humilis', an unostentatious humble style, is the proper mode for a Christian statement.[27] Yet it is also, in this poem, a suspiciously passionless style compared with the riotous efflorescence, high and low, positive and negative, of the material about the world which follows.

The church message is not inherently lively, and it is also basically dual, though not necessarily self-contradictory (as was Aeneas's story in *The Book of Fame*). Scipio's ancestor showed him the value of earthly merit:

> . . . what man, lered other lewed,
> That loved commune profyt, wel ithewed,
> He shulde into a blysful place wende,
> There as joye is that last withouten ende.

> (46–9)

The person who worked for mutual benefit on earth would gain salvation: such secular moralism matches the reputation of Scipio as 'a prototypical temporal leader',[28] but as the precis continues, the world is scorned as 'lyte, And ful of torment and of harde grace' (64–5): Bennett has described in detail the elements of 'dualism' in this sequence.[29]

The narrator is not satisfied: this complex message is not the 'certeyn thing' he sought (20); he comments with disturbed puzzlement in lines which modern editors make improperly smooth (90 in fact lacks 'which' and 91 should lose its first 'that'). So he worries himself to sleep. Before the dream begins, two constant elements of dream poems are offered, but in such offhand ways and at such reduced power that the audience can have little real hope of receiving a confident and problem-resolving dream. The 'dream theory' sequence is no more than a stanza, which merely says that people dream about their daily concerns (99–105): the invocation of Venus is also a single stanza (113–19), hidden away in the body of the poem and, it seems, weakened by an enigmatic and perhaps ironic reference to her appearance in the 'North-north-west'.[30]

As the dream begins, a complex and interwoven duality is asserted.[31] Africanus, Scipio's mentor in the book, pushes the uninvolved dreamer into a park through a gate which has above it conflicting messages. One speaks of the beneficent power of love, as access to 'the welle of grace' (129); the other promises only pain, sterility and death (135–9). The *Roman de la Rose* presented Cupid carrying two sets of arrows, one bright and lively, one dark and deadly. In the period Venus herself and even nature were often seen as having two sides, positive and negative, as Bennett expounds at length.[32] But Chaucer makes a drastic and powerful compression of the possibilities: only one gate into one park must indicate that conflict is unavoidable, that good and bad are inextricably interwoven.

Inside the splendid park, the narrator who knows no love and is only a spectator (social displacement is again the position for analysis) sees symbolic presentations of a conflicted world through a formal list of trees to which Chaucer has added dark connotations from the human context — elms for coffins, holm oaks for whips, yews and aspen for bow and arrows, the fatal weaponry of the contemporary battlefield. But where humans are not found the natural world is benign and beautiful; this is asserted in a lyric sequence of natural harmony whose ideal status is marked by the fact that it exists outside of time — here there is no age or even night (207–10).

Human figures reappear in the context of aristocratic life and the courtly love that was part of its ideological self-validation. In the Temple of Venus sequence (which provides in some manuscripts a title for the poem, as misleadingly selective as 'The House of Fame') Chaucer sums up the essence of the *fin amor* setting and action which he first knew from the *Roman de la Rose* and then found in Boccaccio. This sequence leans heavily on the *Teseida*, but the source is subtly changed to stress a negative impact. Brewer sees 'a hot house of illicit sensuality' and Bennett finds it 'more sultry, more sinister and at the same time more voluptuous' than its original.[33] By selecting and juxtaposing figures like 'Foolhardynesse, Flaterye and Desyr' (227), by stressing the cruel impact of Cupid's arrows, by inflating the role of the prurient, infertile Priapus, by making Venus more a centrefold than a goddess, by shifting the list of love's martyrs to the end, Chaucer makes firmly negative the aristocratic and literary tradition of love.

The dreamer returns briefly to the ideal natural setting, starts off again, and comes to an alternative possibility, the world of benign and powerful Nature, not found in an ornate and artificial human setting but out in the meadows and peopled with birds. The literary reference now is to Alanus de Insulis, not Boccaccio, and the inference is that Alanus's Christian Platonism, will provide a positive and authoritative 'certeyn thing'.[34] A fluent high style implies this as much as the powerful beauty of Nature herself:

> And in a launde, upon an hil of floures,
> Was set this noble goddesse Nature.
> Of braunches were here halles and here boures
> Iwrought after here cast and here mesure;
> Ne there nas foul that cometh of engendrure
> That they ne were prest in here presence,
> To take hire dom and yeve hire audyence.

> (302–8)

Here, it seems, is a female authority finer and more reliable than was Venus or Fame. But this proves hardly true; Nature's power will not order her surroundings but will be employed ideologically to resolve the disorder that develops there, a conflict which is seen to be both basic to animal and human life and also to be a specific late fourteenth century phenomenon.

The birds exist in four classes, as Aristotle and Alanus agreed. The birds of prey sit highest, then come the small birds that eat worms, and lowest of all the water birds; on the grass, and apparently aside from that hierarchy, sit the seed-fowl in huge numbers (323–9). That seems — so far — an unremarkable and unstrained scheme. Then the birds are listed in detail of species, and here enters a strong note of conflict: it is in the nature of many to prey on others or to exhibit negative features, but these are given in distinctly human terms, among them the 'jelous swan', the 'skornynge jay', the 'false lapwynge', the 'coward kyte', and the 'swalwe, motherere of the foules smale' (342–53).

Birds were frequently used in ancient and medieval literature as the medium of statements about men, and while the reality of 'nature red in tooth and claw' is evidently part of the meaning of the list, it tends irresistibly towards human conflict, and that is the impact of the following 'parliament'. It is St Valentine's day (imagined to be in spring, not early February) and the birds have come to choose their mates. Nature invites them to speak in hierarchical order and her orderly power is restated, in lines as weighty and sonorous as Chaucer ever wrote:

> Nature, the vicaire of the almyghty Lord,
> That hot, cold, hevy, lyght, moyst, and dreye
> Hath knyt by evene noumbres of acord.

(379–81)

Three eagles dispute for one fine female eagle: the mode of the sequence is the well-known 'question d'amour', the sort of thing basic to French love allegories, which both elaborated the beauty of courtly love and ultimately asserted the authority of the royal figure who judged the debate.[35] Here, where the aristocratic certainties of *The Book of the Duchess* have been abandoned, neither courtly love or royal authority survive without substantial attack. The eagles speak all day long, so that the lower birds finally break in to have their turn, to receive their rights and 'to ben delivered' (491). They produce representatives to debate the eagles' problem and the elegant process of the love debate turns into a turbulent slanging match between the classes that were previously so calmly mentioned.

The title of the poem, the action of this sequence and the language used all indicate that this is much more than avian farce. The phrase 'to ben delivered' is a technical term for the ending of a parliamentary session; the commons in the medieval parliament had just established the right to elect a speaker; tense confrontation between lords and commons was a marked feature of the 1370s parliaments.[36] In Scipio's dream, conflict was between heaven and earth; it grew between love good and bad in the temple of Venus, but it is now located in a dramatic political tension of Chaucer's own period.

The relationship between the birds' argument and the parliaments of the day is detailed. Nature seems to speak as the chancellor did, opening the parliament for the king; the language is heavily legal in register and so was the conception of 'the high court of parliament'; the commons did debate issues raised by the chancellor and report through their speaker to the lords.[37] Those general resemblances can be made more specific. Careful attention to what happens here and to contemporary events makes it clear that Chaucer is dealing with the most contentious and disturbing of recent parliaments, in which men well known to him were involved and which resonated through the later 1370s.[38]

In 1376 was held what became known as the 'Good Parliament', in which the administration of the ageing Edward III was severely attacked, several of his operatives were displaced and imprisoned and John of Gaunt was distinctly embarrassed. Those achievements were rapidly reversed by the Gaunt-dominated parliament called in January 1377. More important, in the eyes of historians, were the strategic gains made by the commons, and it is these structurally crucial events upon which Chaucer concentrates — a sign of the analytic accuracy of his historical imagination. A distinct self-consciousness and aggression among the commons was evident: previously they had largely gone along, however unwillingly, with royal and aristocratic demands, especially for taxes. In this parliament they first elected a forceful speaker, Sir Peter de la Mare. He insisted that all the commons, not a select committee, should join the lords to debate their problems and the commons' grievances together. From this dramatic occasion arises, it would appear, the stress Chaucer lays on overcrowding (314–15) and chaos in general. This consultative process was known as 'communing', and may lie beneath the cuckoo's insistence on 'comune spede' (507), an evidently ironic version of Scipio's 'commune profyt'.

Looking back to the opening of Nature's scene from this argument, and in the context of the contemporary parliaments, it seems clear that the hierarchy of birds is relevant to the estates of the parliament. The birds of prey represent the lords — all commentators agree on that, though few have seen the essentially unflattering connotations. The seed-fowl who sit to one side in apparent humility but huge numbers and steadfastly, through the turtle dove, support the nobles, must indicate the bishops who regularly attended parliament and were loyal conservatives. Water-fowl and worm-fowl form an uneasy coalition in the birds' debate against the lords, as did the knights from the shires and the urban burgesses in the 'Good Parliament', the two elements of the commons. The comic vigour of the lower birds' performance and the languid selfishness of the higher birds are both negative, like the equally distasteful features of fame and rumour in *The Book of Fame*. The onlooker finds the whole thing distressing, a model of disorder and, it is consistently implied, of unnaturally turbulent conflict.

But unlike *The Book of Fame*, this poem and its conflict are capable of resolution: the observed strains do not disrupt the author's art. Indeed, it is through deployment of art itself that Chaucer finds a resolution. Though Nature recommends the highest eagle 'if it were resoun' (the true reading in 632, and a consistent parliamentary idiom), the female bird, like any much loved courtly lady, asks for time to think. The mechanism of the courtly love tradition is skilfully used with a double impact. It provides a last resemblance to the 'Good Parliament', where the king and lords went without the demanded taxes, but it also brings the tension to an end. And then, in a sudden and simplistic conclusion, all the other birds take their mates 'by evene acord' (668): the notion of God's natural harmony is employed to mask conflict, the only instance of Nature having real power is an ideological device rather than a divine principle at work through the sequence.

The strain of this sudden and patched-up conclusion is, however, itself concealed by a value emergent in the poem — poetic art itself. Harmony may have been imposed rather arbitrarily, but it is enacted in the poetry to make its presence convincing. The rhymes in the resolving stanza (666–72) are unusually close to each other: 'ende/wende' and 'wynde/kynde'. That this is no accident is shown when 'fynde/mynde' ends the next stanza (678–9), and 'synge/ departynge' in 673 and 675 support this unparalleled rhyme-linking. That subtle device introduces the central statement of formal and thematic harmony, as the birds, suddenly all in 'evene acord' (668) sing a parting rondel which states that summer and winter, archetypes of conflict in nature, are themselves only part of a temporally revolving divine and natural pattern. The rondel form revolves around itself; harmony could not be more harmonious.

Art may well stand out further from the detailed surface of the poem as its resolving force, for if the rondel were expanded normally, not as all modern editors have treated it, there would be one more line — 682 should occur again after 686, as even a cursory reading would suggest. Then, the whole poem would have seven hundred lines or, more importantly, a hundred stanzas.[39] That number consistently implied completeness (as in the parable of the sower, to give one very well-known example); the poem that has found true order hard to find on earth would through its own total form assure the audience that, in art at least, harmony is not beyond attainment.

Yet the strain of the sudden ending can hardly be forgotten for all the brilliance of its ideological concealment, and the narrator himself is a final agent of disturbance. In his last remark his old dissatisfaction is restated; he goes back to his books to find that 'certeyn thyng' that has eluded him:

> I hope, ywis, to rede so som day
> That I shal mete some thyng for to fare
> The bet, and thus to rede I nyl nat spare.

(697–9)

Will he *encounter* it in books (Modern English 'meet') or *dream* it after reading (Middle English 'mete')? The language leaves the matter open, a subtler version of the uncertainty that both ends and disrupts *The Book of Fame*. The narrator certainly does not find security in Scipio's dream or in similar Christian material. That type of authority is suspended, treated as another doubtful source of security.

This most closely woven and subtly powerful poem lacks the steep gradients of social conflict and resultant confusion of *The Book of Fame* as surely as it lacks the simple aristocratic confidence of *The Book of the Duchess*. The artist is now in full control of his deeply analytic perceptions, but they are not any less probing, and the imagination is not any less historical. The same artistic powers and the same contemporary analysis will be developed in Chaucer's next major work, *Troilus and Criseyde*, where he turns from an allegorical and theoretical analysis of social conflict to consider in much greater and much more humanly realized detail the conflict of an emerging self-consciousness and a still existing collective concept of people and their society — so developing in full scope and in the humanist possibilities of a narrative mode the issues raised and urgently explored in the course of the dream poems themselves.

But the three dream poems are not trial pieces or nursery slopes before the detailed study of *Troilus and Criseyde* or the vertiginous brilliance of *The Canterbury Tales*. They are a connected series of powerfully analytic works of art that reveal the progress of the poet's experience and the concordant development of his historically attuned imagination. To understand them in their innately historical terms is to make it possible to grasp the complex and dynamic power of Chaucer's later art.

2 *Troilus and Criseyde:* 'Do wey youre barbe'

I Preface

A masterpiece of medieval courtesy, the first psychological novel, a classic account of earthly versus heavenly love — these are major receptions of *Troilus and Criseyde* and a history of cultural attitudes is inscribed in that succession. English renaissance writers like Sidney and Beaumont felt Chaucer provided an elegant and love-centred model that matched their own Italianate and emotive concerns. It was later critics, bringing bourgeois values of characterization, unitarian structure and worldly wisdom into culture, who elevated the novel-like elements of the poem. More recently a priestly caste of American professors has baptized the text in a shower of footnotes and pronounced it devout Christian allegory.

But the existence of history in the text's reception does not conceal the fact that no one has identified the poem as a thoroughly sociohistorical work. Some have recognized the presence of the Trojan war, but have treated it either as a mere projection of the lovers' anguish or, a little more respectfully, as an ironic analogue of their story.[1] The more sharply historical identification between Troy and New Troy, or London, has been noted.[2] A general type of historicity has also been observed: Benson discerns Chaucer's insertion of 'historical plausibility' into Boccaccio's rather blandly atemporal narrative; Patterson describes a near-contemporary reader sensing the 'reality' of the text; Smyser shows how the detailed domestic geography of the poem meshes fully with London architecture of the late fourteenth century; Bloomfield goes deeper in the poem to find 'not only a sense of chronology, but also an acute sense of cultural change'.[3] These observations have not amounted to seeing the poem as a coherent, imaginative treatment of its period. An important movement in that direction has been made by Aers, whose discussion of Criseyde probes deeply into the affective historicity of part of the poem: the essay will be referred to later.[4]

Though the precise date of *Troilus and Criseyde* remains obscure, it was clearly Chaucer's major occupation between the dream poems and *The Canterbury Tales*. Robinson summarizes the issues: 1382–7 seems to be the period in which it was written.[5] In both *The Book of Fame* and *The Parliament of Fowls* the topic of love was used as a medium for argument about social values. In particular, the collective, honour-based structures exemplified in *The Book of the Duchess*, also through the topic of love, were criticized in those poems, theoretically in *The Book of Fame* and imaginatively in *The Parliament of Fowls*. In *Troilus and Criseyde* that conflict is developed not in personified allegory nor through bird-symbolism, but on the more real terrain of human interaction displayed in narrative.

Troilus and Criseyde explores late medieval developments in social structures and values through the painful and puzzled experiences of human beings in a fully developed and deeply probed set of actions, reactions and interactions. The structures of the public life are seen not in grand performance as in Octavian's hunt, the palace of Fame herself or in the temple of Venus, but as they are internalized by people as they constrict and even destroy awakened inner feelings. The dialectical relations of public and private life and values are the central topic of *Troilus and Criseyde*, and the poem is a most potent realization of a structure of feeling in a period when, in a mobile socioeconomic environment, the private sphere was beginning to be constructed as a possible self-concept for human beings.

As has been argued in the previous chapter, the dominant nature of public values is evident throughout the medieval period and its culture is a major means of asserting those values. Spearing has observed them at work in *Troilus and Criseyde*, but like other skilled 'close readers' his purely literary commitment prevents him from developing the social patterns he acutely discerns.[6] Muscatine's use of the social categories of aristocratic and bourgeois in almost completely literary ways is the most striking example of this phenomenon; another is the restricted and cultural scope of Burrow's 'Ricardian' analysis of the period.[7]

The force of honour and public values was in dialectic with a force of privacy. Medieval people did not belive they were actually not separate from each other: theirs was not a ludicrous collective-only ideology — nor is that attitude held today even by such non-individualist people as tribal Australian aborigines. They saw, rather, a crucial tension between the social unit that was necessary for security (both in terms of food production and defence) and the separate people who comprised the crucial togetherness. That tension is one of the major issues of early literature, whether it deals with the need to socialize the warrior hero or to sublimate the drives of physical passion.

The term 'dialectic', in proper use, means that two forces are essentially interwoven, that, for example, the capitalist system which creates mass production in factories also produces the organized labour which is the source of the system's implacable opposition. The structure of honorific relations between men and men had as its inescapably individualistic core the force of 'competitive assertiveness', as the most recent and most specific historian of honour has outlined.[8] Similarly, the courteous relations between men and women, collectivized as *fin amor*, had as an inner motor the private passion of love. The role of chivalric culture was to mask these inner and individualist forces and insist on the ideologically acceptable and socially undisturbing public patterns as both admirable and authentic.

Because of the dialectical character of the official public ideology and its covert private dynamism, it is easy for modern bourgeois ideologues to trace in medieval culture certain elements of individualism. The crucial thrust of their work is to detach bourgeois values from capitalist development and so establish a position from which individualism seems a natural and absolute condition of humanity, not a historically relative phenomenon. The work of Hanning and Dronke in literature, Morris in religion, Macfarlane in sociology and Southern in history is both partial scholarship and potent ideology.[9]

Yet the individualism of twelfth century romance — a central terrain for such writers — is only expressed through collectivized modes: in *Yvain* the hero's private and profitable love is expressed through the power of a generalized figure of 'Love'; the lover of the influential *Roman de la Rose* is no more than a type called *amans*, 'lover', not a young man making his way in the world and the novel. Tristan and Isolde, are, in Gottfried von Strassburg's dominating version, themselves no more than personal sites for the operations of the counter-collective but still generalized force of ideal passion.

The medieval situation is best comprehended as a reverse of the modern pattern when, in a world rich with collective forces (such as democratic politics, computerized information systems and international monopoly capitalism) culture insistently asserts the existence and value of the individual person and his or her values. It is the radical and historically imaginative artist who can cut through an ideological structure and realize the true character of dialectical reality. In the modern period non-representational visual artists have borne the brunt of this enterprise, and their thrust has been followed by writers like Kafka, Beckett, the projects of the French new novel and American experimental poetry.

In *Troilus and Criseyde* Chaucer is working in a similarly ground-breaking way. His lovers are not, like Tristan and Isolde, the repositories of forces which are themselves consolingly collective. His treatment is not entirely and undisturbingly public and traditonal. His adventure is to internalize the conflicts of private and public and to write a romance which actualizes the personal feelings of love in terms of flesh and blood and human speech. This is not a simple matter. The novel is not conceived and born at once: it will depend on a whole structure of social and economic patterns for its full development. What Chaucer does is to show the nature and the value of the private world, and (the crucial historical connection) its inability to survive in a world still public in its concepts of knowing and being and so in its 'social construction of reality' as Berger and Luckmann would put it.[10]

Love, in this new analysis, is no longer a mask for the chivalric ideology of cavalry or the appropriation of property owned by women, as it was in the classic romances,[11] nor is it just a medium throuh which social conflict can be approached, as it was in Chaucer's earlier dream poems. Love here is love as it is now understood, an inescapable attraction between *individual* human beings. But Criseyde is not only a remarkably realized woman, as most readers have thought, not only a step towards feminism.[12] She is a figure of a new self-consciousness for both men and women; it is because women were in so many ways excluded from the authority of a patriarchal public order that Chaucer is able to exploit them as a terrain for the exploration of privacy — the Wife of Bath will be another striking case.

Chaucer's enterprise of the historical imagination in *Troilus and Criseyde* may be seen in two ways, though it operates as a consistent and persuasive force. It is possible to describe in a distanced way the general patterns at work in the poem's construction, and it is also possible to read through the text to show how it realizes in detail the feeling, the force and the counter-force of the private and public worlds. A full account of the poem needs both approaches, and that need itself indicates how the poem operates with both a theoretical grasp of sociocultural patterns and also a deeply imagined recreation of human life. The need for a dual expository technique indicates the transitional nature of the text, transitional not in terms of an arid history of mere literary techniques, but in the sense that the poem brings to complex formal life the historical transitions under way in Chaucer's own particularly dynamic period.

II   General Patterns

Critics have consistently identified conflict in the poem both in terms of form and theme. Many have been content to explain, in a blandly optimistic, consensus-oriented way, how these conflicts resolve themselves: 'Contraries Harmonized in Troilus and Criseyde' is the sub-title of a recent book and it sums up a major critical response and quietist ideology.[13] But other critics have failed to find such a calm resolution. Some see unresolved conflict in itself as central while others, recognizing earthly problems as the prime issue of the narrative, lay stress on the 'epilogue' as a means of resolving on a heavenly level the strains of human life.[14] The following discussion of the general patterns of the text suggests strongly that disharmony, conflict, strain and oppositions of artistic, and so by extension, human and historical forces — these are the elements of the dominant and unresolved pattern of the poem.

The genre of *Troilus and Criseyde* is disturbingly dual. Several critics have identified an 'epic frame' in that it opens and concludes (before the Christian epilogue) in distinctly epic language and attitude.[15] But the bulk of the poem lacks the narrative range, the multiplicity of personnel and incident, the tribal or national standpoint of the epic. In fact the basic story of the poem is extremely slight, and is striking for its extensive treatment of characters' reactions to events: Chaucer often magnifies this from his source. He states firmly at I. 141–7 and V. 1765–71 that this is not an epic of war: it is, rather, a narrow and deep story about people. In genre, that is, the poem is polemical, rejecting the classical and socially conscious form of epic, leaving aside the Troy story for a tale of lovers, just as in the action of the poem the story of Thebes is a marginal presence at Troy, set aside by Criseyde to talk of life and love with Pandarus (II. 81–112) and resumed in the stark prophecies of Cassandra at the end (V. 1450–1533) – both are Chaucerian innovations. For the Trojans the story of Thebes, for the medieval audience the Trojan war, these are marginal and ultimately disturbing presences. That indicates the special, non-public thrust of the poem and also retains in mind the absolute forces of history against which the newly and polemically privatized genre is operating.

Literary structure shows the same sort of dialectical process at work. In terms of large structure, Jordan has argued that the poem is 'Chaucerian Gothic',[16] that is, a work which responds to the aesthetics also found in medieval visual art and allegorical writing, a structure without authoritative internal connections or the single meaningful climax, but steadily working out a set of exemplary episodes which are linked structurally in a 'vertical' way to a higher cultural authority, either God and divinely revealed truth or overarching social verities.[17] This 'Gothic structure' certainly existed as an aesthetic pattern and (less often discerned by critics) as an ideological force which responded to and provided legitimation for a world-view where authority rested with God and his worldly representatives, religious and secular. The structure is clearly visible in *The Book of the Duchess*, and has there an inherently political conservative force.

Yet is is noticeable that after his section on this 'Vertical Structure' Jordan has a longer one on 'Horizontal Structure' confronting and explaining away the many features in the poem which do seem like a post-Gothic pattern, the ways in which characters' speeches and actions are derived from preceding speeches and actions, not from supreme verities, and ways in which the narrative works up in its own terms to a climax full of meaning, as does the classic novel. There are many detailed phenomena of such a 'humanist' technique in the poem, mostly surrounding Pandarus and Criseyde. As a result, Spearing has questioned Jordan's thesis, saying that while the text has Gothic aspects it also reveals a 'strong narrative impetus which drives from scene to scene.'[18] A whole set of artistically unifying correspondences between earlier and later parts of the text give a distinctly un-Gothic feeling to the poem, as Bishop has shown in some detail.[19] Finally, however, the literary structure is also polemical, but this time on behalf of the public world and its co-relative Gothic structure. In the 'epilogue' the text breaks with a novel-like pattern of development and insists on a lurch in the narrative and in the theme, imposing with rigour the vertically and divinely oriented ending.

In the same way the detailed characterization and the literary style which bear the patterns of detailed presentation are also unavoidably dual. The characterization is in part traditional and collective, especially in terms of Troilus and also innovative and forward-looking, especially with reference to Criseyde. These elements of contradictory characterization are set in a context of literary presentation, or 'mimesis', which is notably 'concrete' both in the details of the action and the specifics of time and place.[20] Such patterns of presentation and its conflict are best left to be treated in the later detailed discussion of the text, but they should be recognized as having a general status in the poem, as being a part of the way in which the text constructs a polemical treatment of traditional modes of knowing and being.

Literary style is a major site of conflict in the poem, as Muscatine has established.[21] He distinguishes between Troilus's formal, romance-like manner and Pandarus's much more colloquial and inherently bourgeois style, with Criseyde sharing both styles. Muscatine's analysis has literary limits: in fact, the variations of style relate not so much to generic patterns of romance or fabliau, as he sees it, but to the social register of utterance, whether it creates shared values embodied in language (which may be high or low, allegorical or proverbial) or whether a personal and informal utterance is being marked out for value, so creating a new and anti-public discourse of the sort which Halliday calls a 'social semiotic'.[22] These patterns are also discussed in detail below; they are very important for the creation of a public world exhausted of value — and a possibly valid private domain.

The title of the poem itself is in some conflict. It is referred to in the Retractions to *The Canterbury Tales* as 'The Book of Troilus', much as *Tristan* is the normal medieval title of the Tristan and Isolde story. Yet several manuscripts call it by both the lovers' names, and it was referred to in that way by Lydgate in his *Fall of Princes*. The emergent force of Criseyde as a figure seems to demand that description. Chaucer says in his first line that 'the double sorwe' of Troilus is the topic of his poem, but effectively it comes to have a double viewpoint on love and tragedy — a pattern discussed in terms of genre by McAlpine, who suggests it is both a Boethian tragedy about Criseyde and a Boethian comedy based on Troilus.[23]

These general areas of discussion present a consciously polemical work, opposing in each case traditional medieval patterns with more recent and more humanist elements, giving them great force but finally containing them in a peremptory way within traditional patterns. That itself testifies to the power of Chaucer's art and his historical imagination; the craft with which that complex was constructed and the conscious nature of his insight into his period can be seen by comparing his work with its source.

C. S. Lewis said Chaucer 'medievalized' Boccaccio, making Troilus more courtly and noble, revelling in serious features like Troilus's speech on free will and predestination in IV. 958–1078.[24] But, against Lewis's argument, Chaucer also inserted some of the most strikingly quasi-humanist sequences, like most of the long Book II interchanges centred on Criseyde and Pandarus (II. 78–595 and 1093–1302) and most of the long and unforgettable sequence in which Troilus and Criseyde are brought to bed together in Book III (50–217 and 484–1309). Rather than simply medievalizing the poem, Chaucer socialized it. The Italian renaissance artist Boccaccio was able to position himself as a sufficient source for his work and to deal without any sense of conflict in terms of personal feeling: that is why the Italian material provided so rich a source for sixteenth century writing, when the poet as artist-hero and the individual as a self-sufficient terrain of art were culturally rooted in the fuller development of bourgeois social and economic structures.

Chaucer, working in a society less bourgeois and so less individualist in tendency, introduced aspects of medieval collectivity to his source and also created long sequences of brilliant

dialectic between the emergent private world and that newly re-
established public world. The point has been acutely seen,
though not developed, by Windeatt, who has the most recent and
probably the best understanding of just what Chaucer did to his
source:

> Chaucer consistently draws a society that allows much less
> privacy to his lovers, while at the same time he gives to his
> characters a much increased sense that their love affair
> must be secret . . . In *Troilus and Criseyde* the private life of
> the individual still has to be won from a surrounding
> society, and this emphasizes the difference between the
> private and public lives of Chaucer's characters more
> sharply than in *Il Filostrato*.[25]

A sense of socialization is conveyed through the poem by
references to an audience of lovers. This is an evident fiction;
many have thought the poem was directed to the royal court, and
one of the manuscripts seems to show Chaucer reading it in such
a setting. But that illustration is itself a fictional convention and
the core audience seems to be the same as that for *The Book of
Fame* and *The Parliament of Fowls*, namely the intelligentsia of the
court and professional London — two of whom are named at the
very end, John Gower and Ralph Strode (V. 1856–7). Another
view of the audience is that it is fully imagined within the poem —
as fictional lovers, that is, and that the poem is artistically self-
supporting as a result.[26] That would reveal a radically innovative
self-confidence in a work of art, but one that is not inconsistent
with the role of art in *The Parliament of Fowls* or the structural
developments of this poem. It would seem that even in its
relations to an audience, *Troilus and Criseyde* is in conflict between
traditional and new patterns.

III 'Fro wo to wele'

Crucial as all these general and polemical polarities are in the
poem, their essential role is to make possible and powerful its
primary impact, which is the detailed creation of a dominant and
new structure of feeling in the period. The true force of *Troilus and
Criseyde* lies in the intimate, detailed and fully convincing creation
of the human experience of society in a process of change, of
values in a state of crisis and of human beings confronting the

history of their period in terms of their own lives. Only a detailed analysis of a series of passages can convey adequately the depth and power of the poem's historical imagination.

Book I of *Troilus and Criseyde* is dominated by Troilus himself. The opening lines assert that his 'double sorwe' and his tragedy are to be the topic of the poem (I. 1–7, 54–6). The narration moves swiftly through the war setting (I. 57–63) and establishes its impact on Criseyde, abandoned by her skilled, opportunistic and so individualist father. His actions and her problems are treated in some detail, implying that the focus of the poem is on people, not the state or other generalizations, and this is confirmed when the narrator dismisses the topic of war (I. 141–2). Stress is laid on Criseyde's difficult social position, and how she appeals to Ector for new masculine protection in her father's absence. Before the hero makes his appearance in the poem that is ostensibly about himself, two crucial thematic issues are established: the marginality of the war and the danger of solitary existence.

When Troilus appears he is a fully feudal figure. Lewis drew attention to his 'medieval' character and Windeatt has more precisely described Chaucer's amplification of a 'feudal sense' about Troilus.[27] Like any baron he leads a band of young knights and deplores any tendency to desert the collective group for the private pursuits of love. He is a model of the noble life, 'The worthiest and grettest of degree' (I. 244), both 'proud' and 'debonaire' (I. 214). But this position, and the status of such positions, is to be put under question.

As he sees Criseyde, Troilus is 'astoned', thunderstruck with love. But he manages to look at her only sidelong, 'in thrifty wise', then he sighs softly 'lest men myghte hym here' and 'caughte ayeyn his firste pleyinge chere' (I. 274–5 and 279–80). At once his inner feeling is concealed within his public demeanour. But this is not the only, and far from the most expansive, element of public/private conflict in this passage. Criseyde's actual person and Troilus' reaction to it are couched in quite different modes of writing, the one remarkably realistic and even humanist in impact, the other fully medieval and allegorical. First, the text realizes her as a living woman:

> She nas nat with the leste of hire stature,
> But alle hire lymes so wel answerynge

> Weren to wommanhod, that creature
> Was nevere lasse mannysh in semynge.
>
> (I. 281–4)

At once a noticeable and feminine woman, she is subtly enclosed in patriarchal discourse by being redefined as a quite unmanlike, and then that original flicker of unruly naturalism is contained within ideal values:

> And ek the pure wise of hire mevynge
> Shewed wel that men myght in hire gesse
> Honour, estat, and wommanly noblesse.
>
> (I. 285–7)

The phrase the 'pure wise of hire mevynge' stresses her mobile body but that specific sensuality is withdrawn into the public virtues of a noble, woman-dominating class and its idealistic ideology by the structure of honour, estate and, even if it is only womanly, 'noblesse' itself. The strategy of this single stanza indicates Chaucer's apprehension of Criseyde as a human and physical woman enclosed in a world of men and public values: the text will develop at subtle and memorable length that initial characterization.

Troilus is also created as an epitome of his later meaning, his essence caught in a complex of language and implication. At first he reacts physically, himself moved by 'her mevynge and hir chere' (I. 289), but at once this stimulus is subsumed into formal language, the conventional idealism of *fin amor*, which deals not in human physicality but in allegorical analysis:

> And of hire look in him ther gan to quyken
> So gret desir and such affeccioun,
> That in his hertes botme gan to stiken
> Of hir his fixe and depe impressioun.
>
> (I. 295–8)

Their instinctive rapport, central to the plot but a threat in terms of public order and its cultural mode, is idealized away into the statement that 'Love hadde his dwellynge Withinne the subtile stremes of hir yen.' (I. 304–5)

If the reality of physical stimulus is sublimated in this way, the long sequences of Book I that deal with Troilus's response to love construct a similar pattern, but one that essentially questions that medieval public containment and suggests the reality and validity of individual responses. Troilus now pretends to be his honorific public self, even though he is inwardly lovestruck: the statement itself locates reality internally (I. 324–5). At the same time, while he embarks on a long and classic sequence of *fin amor* statements, greatly amplified and 'medievalized' by Chaucer, he is nevertheless revealed as a suffering private person. Instead of losing his troublesome individualism as Man in Black did in that collective culture, Troilus's conflict is painfully emphasized by the process.

He speaks in the formalized language of medieval *fin amor*, as at I. 344–50: he deploys the resources of language and response that transmuted the urgent privacy of passion into an acceptably collective set of responses and created as supervisor and controller of this world a lord with absolute power, the God of Love. And since love is a model of the conservative medieval authority structure, he has like his secular baronial counterparts a collective and faithful body of retainers, those 'loveres' whom Troilus has now joined (I. 344).

Although this language and attitude, sustained by Troilus throughout the book, projects the state of lover in a fully feudal and conservative way, his actual position is consistently outlined as anti-social and so disruptive. The fact that he spends his time alone in his bedroom, is, like Man in Black's initial position, an essential cue. But Troilus's own language bears the message too; a set of highly conventional images of the courtly lover do no more than state the counter-conventional fact that by adopting a private position he is, from a public viewpoint, both degraded and dehumanized. The collective language does not work for him: as a lover he is not, unlike Yvain or Tristan, able to apostrophize convincingly a potent new order. Love, through his fragments of lover's language appears as a socially turbulent problem for him. His lovesong (I. 400–20) is a set of painful contradictions – drinking and thirst, 'swete harm' and 'quikke deth'. Love leaves him desperately isolated: he feels himself 'Al sterelees withinne a boot' (I. 416), an ultimate image of helplessness, used in Old English poetry of that desperate solitary, the lordless man. Troilus has no more status than a trapped bird when 'love bigan his fetheres so to lyme' (I. 353); in human terms he is love's serf and, to make the matter humiliatingly clear, the fire of love 'brende hym so' he lost his aristocratic leisured pallor and looked like a ruddy churl (I. 435–

41). Alone, desocialized, dehumanized, he is no more than a captive beast who can only 'gnaw thin owen cheyne' (I. 509).

Just as Criseyde's human uniqueness was touched in and quickly withdrawn under the veil of public language and values, so Troilus's actual private relations with her are constantly alluded to but never confronted in their own terms. He is collapsed, in secret, unable even to verbalize what his problem is, speaking in a code that provides only implicit criticisms of his status through metaphorics that delineate the absence of both language and feeling of privacy. Troilus is not only a ruin of a noble man, but also of public language and public self-concepts.

When he returns to his lonely room, Troilus is 'langwisshinge' (I. 569); Pandarus arrives but he refuses to speak (I. 722–3) or to explain his trouble (I. 752–60), blaming it on the ultimate faceless force of Fortune (I. 834– 40). But Pandarus manages to press him, through insistent fellowship and offers of fraternal help, to externalize himself enough to reveal the source of his despair. Pandarus is Troilus's friend and says he too is a lover. By a whole set of what Lumiansky has called 'proverbial monitory elements',[28] scraps of elementary public wisdom, and by insisting that Troilus is not alone in his disrupted state, Pandarus learns the problem and promises to correct it: he is not only friend to Troilus but uncle to Criseyde and so ideally placed, socially, to resolve the matter. As a result Troilus is able again to resume his honorific self: he 'pleyde the leoun' (I. 1074) against the Greeks, and cut once more a baronial figure in the city, the language oozing with feudal codewords;

> For he bicom the frendlieste wight,
> The gentilest, and ek the mooste fre,
> The thriftiest and oon the beste knyght
> That in his tyme was or myghte be.

> (I. 1079–82)

If Troilus is in this way a figure of the public world thrown into private disorder, the role of Pandarus is important to assess. Is he an agent of the public world, bringing its skills and values to bear on private anxiety and dispel it entirely, so leading Troilus to a shared and public love fit to match his public honour? That was the structure that operated through and over the narrator in *The Book of the Duchess*. Or is Pandarus a more realistic figure of the manipulative fixing that operated in and around the public world so that its figures should have just what they privately wanted in their 'competitive assertiveness' and never suffer their valuable honour to be breached? The threadbare proverbial character of Pandarus's language and the frenetic insistence of his helpfulness suggests the latter, negative role, but his position will not become clear until his part has been played out in full in the context of Criseyde and her responses, a process which dominates Book II.

In that Book Chaucer has made several crucial alterations to her character. A simple one has elevated her social status: here she has a 'paleys' (II. 76), not the house that Boccaccio gave her. While she is still not Troilus's equal, having no royal blood, her wealth, position and cultural subtlety are within his own sphere and so their rapport is a serious matter, not dismissable as a mere slumming episode for him. Furthermore, her consistent concern for her own status and honour is no exaggerated arriviste fantasy. More wide-ranging is the change Chaucer has made to Criseyde's whole treatment. There was a widely-known tradition of her as a treacherous lover well before he wrote.[29] The change Chaucer makes to this is not one of action — she still does what she used to do — but only of presentation and interpretation. He gives Criseyde so much of a speaking part and viewpoint and explains so fully the environment of her actions that she and they are fully comprehended and, as a result, much harder to judge in harsh and simplistically traditional terms.

A number of critics have appreciated and explored Chaucer's special and experimental treatment of Criseyde. Lambert suggested that Books I to III have a 'Criseydan' viewpoint; Bishop expressed the same notion by calling her 'a centre of consciousness'; Muscatine outlined lucidly the expansion of her role. These writers see a broadening of poetic scope and human sympathy as the basis of Chaucer's treatment of Criseyde.[30] However, critics such as Fries and Aers have seen Chaucer as speaking for a proto-feminism. Delany has been less impressed and specifies Criseyde's own limitations; by implication Diamond takes the same position, finding the Wife of Bath Chaucer's only real feminist figure.[31] They are right to be cautious; Chaucer is not so much creating a female position in its own right as exploiting the fact that women did not share in feudal and patriarchal power. He is, however, using a woman as a position from which to explore the possibility that intrigued him and was historically most dynamic, namely that of private values. This is inherently the case in the Wife of

Bath's tale as well, where female interests are partly elided into anti-aristocratic concerns.

The drama of love creates an essentially anti-social force, and this is the dynamic model through which Chaucer explores a world of conflicting public and private values. In Book I Troilus has served only as a vehicle to outline in its absence the reality of personal feeling and private reality, but in Book II the essentially unpowerful voice of a woman is used as a medium to realize both a human self-consciousness and a kind of art, both of which are opposed to the collective coercions of the medieval public world. Being a medieval woman of some social standing, Criseyde is well aware of the power and value of the outer and public world: she is actually listening to a book about the Theban war when Pandarus arrives, but he, in a typically Chaucerian opening motif, rich with future significance, invites her to think about modern life and love:

> But lat be this, and telle me how ye fare.
> Do wey youre barbe, and shewe your face bare;
> Do wey youre book, rys up and lat us daunce,
> And lat us don to May some observaunce.

(II. 109–12)

Through Criseyde, Chaucer does indeed let drop the 'barbe', or veil of public behaviour and set aside the book of collective wisdom and language; his own language indicates his consciousness of the adventure on which he is embarked to realize love in the terms of instinctive vigour rather than the bookish and ideologically veiled language of *fin amor*.

Criseyde a socially conscious widowed lady, feels Pandarus is 'wylde' (II. 116), a damning epithet in terms of social and cultural order. Such conventional judgements are not forced upon her: she has thoroughly internalized public standards; unlike the poem itself, she thinks a lot about the war (II. 124), she sees the proper role of a prince as being an honourable leader in battle (II. 164) and accordingly, when her uncle invites her to reflect on Troilus, she sees him only in his public persona as a noble prince, second to his older brother Hector (II. 183). Impeccably public as these responses are, she does not share fully in that world, and is distinctly uneasy about it. When she does think of the war, she is 'of Grekes so fered that I deye' (II. 124) and her relationship with Ector has been already shown as highly apprehensive, that of a vulnerable private person. Accordingly, when she contemplates love, her reaction is that it may bring her public discredit: 'What men wolde of it deme I kan nat seye.' (II. 461)

Although she is oppressed by the public world and its pressures, she is not thrown into dysfunctional passivity by the privatizing impact of love, and that is because she possesses or has developed resources in the private domain. Her father Calchas was a striking example of a pure individualist: because he knew the Trojans would lose, he left Troy and all the social kudos and material effects he owned there. The language of the poem itself has stigmatized him for this, using a deliberately mocking and belittling tone — 'This Calchas knew by calkulynge' (I. 71) is the first example, but they run throughout his presentation.[32] His daughter may be 'the ferfulleste wight That myghte be' (II. 450–1), but this is because she recognizes problems; she is also a person of private status and strength. She worries what people will think (II. 461), and therefore concludes 'It nedeth me ful sleighly for to pleye' (II. 462) and decides she is capable of organizing things satisfactorily:

> I shal so doon, myn honour shal I kepe
> And ek his lif

(II. 468–9)

Not only can she see, value and confront public pressure, as was shown by her courage in visiting Ector, she can penetrate and criticize the way in which Pandarus approaches her. His mostly mendacious sequence establishes Troilus in his public role — first mentioned in a blaze of public epithets as 'the kynges deere son . . . The noble Troilus' (II. 316–9) — and then threatens all sorts of public disaster, including Troilus's death and his own, if she is unresponsive. Criseyde answers the question hanging over from Book I about Pandarus's status when she pithily describes this whole manipulative rigmarole as a 'paynted proces' (II. 424). Chaucer has established in her a private intelligence, a capacity to describe tellingly the force of public language and values upon an individual member of a social order. Criseyde's status as a private figure has been described at subtle length by Aers, summing it up as showing:

> Chaucer's interest in the processes of interaction between individual consciousness and various social pressures, manipulations and values, often bewilderingly conflicting.[33]

Pandarus insists on secrecy; he interrupts her social reading party to talk to her when he first arrives; on his second visit he draws her into explicit privacy (II. 1115) and then manoeuvres her into a bizarrely secret meeting with Troilus among a crowd of people at Deiphebe's house. But the poem shows that whereas Troilus is only adrift in that privacy, she is at home in such a state. After Pandarus leaves she spends a long time thinking to herself in a lucid and competent fashion (II. 598–609). Then, while sitting alone at a window, she sees Troilus pass on his way back from fighting. This noble, courageous and real spectacle impresses her deeply:

> Criseyda gan al his chere aspien,
> And leet it so softe in hire herte synke
> That to hireself she seyde, 'Who yaf me drynke?'
>
> (II. 649–51)

She acknowledges her physical stimulation in a self-assured and solitary way.

There are two major significances of this moment. Firstly, her feeling for Troilus is established by herself, within herself. Pandarus's complex manipulations, past and future, are not necessary: he soon arranges for a deliberate staging of a Troilus-viewing with him present as commentator and pressuring presence (II. 1185–1302), but she already knows where she stands, just as the narrator in *The Book of Fame* knew what he though about Fame and her entourage. Criseyde's essential being and knowing is inward and private. Secondly, and for literary history more strikingly, the method of this scene and the establishment of Criseyde are in a mode much more like the modern novel than the inherently allegorical mode of medieval romance. The scene does not, for example, say she saw Love sit in Troilus's noble frame; it charts a human and physical response to another person. Critics have found the elements of the psychological novel in this poem, because Chaucer adventures in that direction, but it is important to see that this is a sequence of highly polemical art. Such core moments of privatized reality are the high points of Chaucer's experiment towards a humanized narrative, and they are not allowed to stand with total authority. Immediately afterwards Criseyde reacts with anxiety towards this revealed inner feeling. Will she lose the sense she has of being 'free', of being in socioeconomic self-confidence her 'owene womman' (II. 771 and 750)? Considering his outward honour (II. 736–40) and her own reflected glory as his woman (II. 705–7), she also sees the threat of public penalties that will come from such a love (II. 708–14). Fear of shame and public disturbance act out the oppressions of public life upon the private, assured person she essentially is, and she is left in doubt, 'Now hoot, now cold' (II. 811).

Unable as she is to argue her private way to a sure conclusion, it is clear that the inner world is not even in her case self-sufficient; it is rather a threatened and perilous estate. A publicized version of the private mode is required to calm her anxieties; she hears Antigone sing about the nobility of love, generating the idea of a selfless community of lovers. The collectivized language of love, that in Troilus's case only gave fragmentary statements of dysfunction, now acts as an external balm. So Criseyde sleeps, to dream of the exchange of hearts in love, a rationalizing image of an intimate community, a way to conceive of the private world of love in quasi-collective terms.

The remainder of Book II treats in belittlingly miniscule detail Pandarus's increasingly complicated and artificial process of manipulation: Troilus is paraded in letters, down the street and in various invented states, then finally come the anti-social social machinations to bring the lovers to an intensely strained private meeting at Deiphebus's house. Criseyde goes along with all this, making sure the public forms are always recognized and enacted, but basically following Pandarus because she is, as the text has in its novel-like inner relevations made clear, already committed. Because of that, the actions of Pandarus are all the more evidently a 'paynted proces'. The public sphere is shown to be more and more inauthentic as the reader, like the two lovers, awaits with mounting frustration the moment of real implied value, when the lovers can enact fully their love in an untrammelled and unpressured private world.

Book III begins with a famous hymn to love, taken by Chaucer from the mouth of Boccaccio's Troilo later in the action of this book. Literary critics have often seen this as a valid praise of earthly love, to match and in some way counterbalance the final praise of heavenly love in the epilogue. The unobserved point is that this proem operates in fully idealistic and feudal terms, and so makes all the more cramped, difficult and temporary the development and enjoyment of a genuinely private and physical love which occurs in this book. The proem is a polemic for high medieval order, power and conservatism, much more powerful than Troilus's unproductive rehearsing of *fin amor* or Pandarus's cynical parroting of it. The proem says of love 'Ye folk a lawe han set in universe', raising *fin amor* beyond chivalric ideology to the status of fixed order, which is seen to 'holden regne and hous in unitee' (III. 36 and 29). Against this, the events of the following book will seem all the more startling, personal and impermanent. The text is realizing its own containment before it gives cause for any foreclosure; the retaliation is put in first.

Book III's action opens in a radically private setting, the social hole-in-corner manipulated into being by Pandarus's frenetic policing of the company's movements at Deiphebe's house. Before any speech between Troilus and Criseyde, their relationship is sealed: though she asks for his protective lordship in feudal language he, in collapse, cannot answer (III. 80), and she is committed personally to him in equal silence:

> For she was wis, and loved hym nevere the lasse,
>
> (III. 86)

The true exchange, that is, is more private than even a narrator can indicate, though Chaucer moves a good way towards the position of the omniscient novel-narrator to indicate their deep-laid unity.

Society returns to their world, and imposes severe strains on them as no more than 'oon and two' (III. 193–4). The narrator stresses, even relishes, the sheer difficulty of intimacy:

> Lest any wight devynen or devyse
> Wolde of hem two, or to it laye an ere,
> That al this world so leef to hem ne were
> As that Cupide wolde hem grace sende
> To maken of hire speche aright an ende.
>
> (III. 458–62)

Critics have often fretted about all this secrecy: why did they not marry, or why could she not be his avowed mistress? This is to be weighed down with rationalistic chains. The secrecy is the central thing, and the lovers form a convincing medium for its existence. It is the hunted character of the private life and private values that Chaucer is primarily realizing. These are deeply compromised values as well, without their own capacity to stand in their own right; in order to be alone together, the lovers have to go through a whole series of awkward and even shabby arrangements at Pandarus's hands.

Troilus is summoned to his house and enclosed within a 'stewe': religious-minded critics (of whom there is a surprising number) read 'brothel' as the implication, but Chaucer has in mind the reduction of the noble prince to the level of a serf or thrall, as his own hysterical imagery foresaw in Book I. Criseyde is brought to Pandarus's house by yet more 'paynted proces', this time his insistence that Troilus is 'out of towne' (III. 570) and because of the enormous storm she is forced to stay. But before that can occur, Criseyde's constant anxiety about dishonour must be allayed by Pandarus's arrangements and mendacity. His previous tall tale to entrap Criseyde had been an external fantasy about loss of property (II. 1415–84). Now he tells a quite private fable about Troilus's jealousy of a certain Horaste. The terrain of discourse has shifted and so has the character of the action. Before, Troilus lay passive and Criseyde was inveigled in through a lively social crowd. Here no onlookers are awake and it is Troilus who appears through a trap in the floor, a moment that stresses the fantastic difficulty of such a union. Pandarus's bizarre actions in running about, stripping Troilus's shirt and pushing him into bed indicate not so much the inherent sinfulness of this whole performance as Troilus's innate inability to act in this mode.

Throughout the sequence Criseyde insists on the maintenance of her honour, just as she fretted about its delicacy and her attendant loss of personal liberty when she debated in Book II whether to enact her instinctive love for Troilus. She wants to call 'som wight' when she hears Troilus has arrived (III. 760), but because Pandarus swears he came in total secrecy (III. 789) and because she trusts them to arrange everything to save her honour (III. 941–45) she accepts that Troilus may have his harmless 'pleasaunce' — but still wants to get up. Criseyde accepts as valid Pandarus's public manipulations; she is alarmed for Troilus's notional jealousy and makes a strongly felt affectionate speech about her fidelity to him (III. 988–1054). Genuinely private as she is, she still believes in and operates according to the dominant external values.

All the while the quasi-public Pandarus has been edging closer to the intensely private goal that he describes in grotesquely public terms: 'For soone hope I we shul ben alle merye' (III. 952). Criseyde's feeling for Troilus, her inner probity and her imposed maintenance of traditional public values have all been deeply tested in this disturbing sequence. Troilus, the private lover but inflexibly public man, is inarticulate and beyond action in this sphere, unable like her to operate between the two domains of value. He can only be acted for by Pandarus, who pays no more than lip-service to external values. The real character of *fin amor* from the male viewpoint is revealed at its worst, as no more than a set of appropriative manipulations; the real value of Criseyde's true inner feeling is manifest. A 'barbe' has indeed been dropped, but it bares the shameful behaviour of he patriarchal order rather than any disgraceful privacy in Criseyde.

As a new example of his dysfunction, caught between a public world he cannot value and a private world he cannot enact, Troilus faints. He is brought round by Criseyde, both physically and with a penetrating statement of private reality: 'Now speke to me, for it am I, Criseyde' (III. 1112). Then as he wakes she takes the lead:

> And therwithal hire arm over hym she leyde,
> And al foryaf, and ofte tyme hym keste.
>
> (III. 1128–9)

In truly intimate pillow-talk about what has occurred between them, with Pandarus finally withdrawing, Criseyde, in a statement that cuts through all the rigmarole and scheming, makes clear to Troilus what the audience has long known — that she is privately and generally committed to him. He replies, with a newly assumed masculine confidence now the private domain is actually before him, 'Now yeldeth yow, for other bote is noon'. She answers with telling wisdom and resource:

> 'Ne hadde I er now, my swete herte deere,
> Ben yold, ywis, I were now nought heere.'
>
> (III. 1210–11)

The narrator comments, 'O sooth is seyd' — and then goes on to hide the inner meaning of the comment in one of his own 'proverbial monitory elements' (III. 1212–18).

Even though Criseyde has thoroughly internalized the values

of a public world, borne them before her consciously in the previous part of the crucial scene, these can be put to rest in conditions of extreme secrecy; even though Troilus has no aptitude at all for the private life, he can be brought, with his mediator's connivance and his lover's commitment, to the point of real intimacy. The human enactment of love, its realization in specific and individual terms, is now before the poet, and he does not fail to develop the scene in powerful, tender and erotic detail. As Bishop aptly comments.[34] Criseyde, who first appeared in the formal guise of widow, is now described in the private glory of a nude (III. 1247–50). The poem avoids the conventional, language of *fin amor* as it was used in Book I and the idealistic conservatism of love-allegory, except to reject its terms, as in III. 1373–9, lines which firmly state the existential validity of such an intimate exchange.

So the core of the poem, in structural terms and in its narrative movement, has driven inward and inward, into a tiny secret room in a blinding rainstorm, into the secret feelings and lives of the two major characters. What has become a commonplace of the novel and the film is here a potently polemical statement of human experience and is given a realized value that opposes all the forces that surround it, social, Christian, allegorical and political — political both in terms of medieval structures of human life and, in this story, of the progress of the war.

Lovers traditionally wake to abuse the dawn; so much is called a convention by scholars who fail to see that patterns only become conventional through their dynamic meaning. The weight this convention bears is deeply social. Darkness makes possible private relations; the sun is their enemy, a public tell-tale:

> O cruel day, accusour of the joie
> That nyght and love han stole and faste iwryen,
> Acorsed be thi comyng into Troye
> For every bore hath oon of thi bryght yen.

> (III. 1450–3)

The sun has entered the city, every crack and knot-hole is a potential accuser, a bearer of public odium. The aubade is developed at length and with unusual weight in the woman's

part,[35] appropriately for this unusually self-assertive and self-
conscious woman. Then the lovers separate, never again to enjoy
in fully recreated form their private community of love.

Troilus returns to his palace and his desolate room; later he
will meet Criseyde again, sing his song to love, and fight well —
but only for his lady's sake. The strangely bleak final stanzas
about Troilus in Book III are stripped of the warm intimacy of
the great love scene. They suggest nothing more than a public
prince operating a reasonably successful and innocuous private
love affair; this cool presentation predicts the failure of their
private world to maintain itself.

With Criseyde, though, the treatment is different. The mode of
novel-like intimacy and suggestive action continues. As Pandarus
comes into the bedroom the morning after, a famously naturalistic
scene occurs. He asks if she would like to kill him, then kisses her
and asks how she is. She replies:

> . . . 'Nevere the bet for yow,
> Fox that ye ben! God yeve youre herte kare!
> God help me so, ye caused al this fare,
>
> (III. 1564–6)

Then she blushes, and hides her head under the sheet.

Intimate realism, a sense of depth beneath the action and
words, a glimpse into inner feelings and motivations are all richly
conveyed here. For a moment, the mode of the novel is
completely mastered, an inner reality shows the tip of its depths
in outward gesture and speech. Criseyde lives in that world now
as she previously did, however much she knows about the need to
feel shame and hide the private person. Troilus is still the figure
of the public world, confronting privacy as a delightful but
mysterious and even troublesome possibility. This is presumably
why Chaucer takes from his mouth the powerful praise of love,
which (as the proem to Book III) realized in sensual depth and
detail the actualized as well as the generalized power of love. The
speech that he is given (III. 1744–71) is entirely general and
Troilus hopes that the God of Love will make everybody, by force
if necessary (III. 1765–9), into lovers. His appreciation of his new
position is hardly one of private joy: he transmutes it into an
imaginary collective state.

IV 'after out of joie'

In a total change of mode as well as a novel-like turn in plot and meaning, Book IV begins with a brisk and stark proem about Fortune and what will happen; the narrative itself opens with the war and atttendant problems. The margins of this story have suddenly swarmed across the page. Antenor has been taken by the Trojans; Calchas wants to ameliorate his isolation among the Greeks and exchange his daughter for Antenor, Troilus's brother. The most dominant public spheres of all, war and family, have erupted into the life of the lovers. Fortune is to blame, says the proem, directly from Boccaccio (IV. 1–7). There are many references to Fortune as a force in the text, but they tend to be in the mouth of the despairing Troilus and they tend to gather in the final stages of the action. Chaucer makes the blame laid on Fortune rather peremptory and indeed seem something of an inauthentic mystification, as Aers has noted.[36]

The forces most obviously at work in the poem are the constricting pressures of the public sphere and they become specific through Chaucer's insertion of a lengthy account of the parliament which decides to exchange Criseyde in spite of Ector's noble statement that 'We usen here no women for to selle' (IV. 182). This has been seen as a reference to the parliament of 1386 in which Chaucer sat and where much damage was done to his friends and even to himself.[37] There certainly seems to be some linking of this Trojan parliament to the extremism of the Peasants' Revolt (IV. 183–4) and Anderson may be right to see this as a treatment of the state of English policy at the time.[38] But the strongest impact of the poem here is general, not specific, a sense that the exterior world has come surging back as a force just when a real and valued privacy had been established.

The actions of the lovers set out their own positions and meanings in the long-developed public/private conflict. Troilus, as a newly experienced and confirmed private lover, hates the idea of losing his 'herte' but his position, to which he returned fully at the end of Book III, and his consciousness, unchanged throughout, will not allow him to do anything of a public character to prevent her going – because her going is, undoubtedly, a public good. The only thing he can conceive of is to act fully privately, to overturn the whole state of affairs by abducting Criseyde, going to his friends and living on his wealth in a totally, even desperately, private state.

This Criseyde refuses to do. She lays stress on his resultant loss of honour, some weight on her loss of name as well (IV. 1555–82). She thinks she can arrange matters so that she will be able to return, and so, she hopes, satisfy the public need and also continue their covert life together after a brief interval. This was just the flexible mode of her behaviour and attitudes in Book II. Troilus's behaviour is also consistent, in that he is so locked into the public mode as a way of life that only its total overthrow can relieve him from it. Unable to believe in an intimate reality within the interstices of public life, unable to manipulate from an honest basis like Criseyde or from a complete lack of principle like Pandarus, he is now a victim of the system as much as she has always been, or more so, because of his lack of previous experience of its oppressive character.

In a sequence that critics have often fretted over, he goes to a temple and speaks his thoughts in the notorious 'predestination and free will' speech (IV. 953–1079). Neither an afterthought by Chaucer, as Windeatt has shown,[39] nor a piece of comedy as some have thought, the fact that this speech never mentions Criseyde and his love both states its strained character and indicates the essential sociohistorical mode of operation of the poem. Overtly Troilus considers the commonly argued medieval problem whether people really have free will or whether, because God has foreknowledge how they will choose to act (as Christian dogma insists) they are in fact thoroughly predetermined. But Troilus is no theologian; Chaucer is using the only intellectual means available to him in theorize the social conflict that his historical imagination has raised to consciousness through the medium of a love story. Publicly operating humans, the story is telling its audience, do not have absolute control of their affairs; collective values do control behaviour. The glimpse of truly free will, like the blissful privacy of a secret passion, is a potent force, but a temporary one, and the real patterns of medieval socialization have to be faced, as Book IV has insisted through its action.

Chaucer did not have access to the theorizations of bourgeois ideology, nor the techniques of sociology: he does very well to realize his complex analysis with the tools to hand, love poetry, various types of narrative modality, theological analysis. The speech he found in Boethius that glumly confronted a type of determinism was answered by Lady Philosophy in genial terms of ultimate Christian freedoms beyond the earth; that point will come up as an 'epilogue' to the poem. Here it is omitted, not because Troilus is a 'slave to his desire', as a doctrinaire Christian reading would have it,[40] but because the topic here is earthly, and that is not only how it looks on earth, it is how, in a public mode of social values, things actually are. Which is not to say that such values are uncritically admired within the poem: Lockhart has shown how the language of 'honour' is steadily devalued throughout the text,[41] and the plot and its implications have made that critique of the public world quite evident.

The lovers have their last meeting, a bitter-sweet private encounter, and insist hopefully that in their exchange of hearts they have constructed a private communality of sorts. Criseyde makes her last, perhaps most potent and prophetic statement of internal reality. She states that it was not Troilus's public position that moved her to love:

For trusteth wel, that youre estat roial,
Ne veyn delit, nor only worthinesse
Of yow in werre or torney marcial,
Ne pompe, array, nobleye, or ek richesse
Ne made me to rewe on your destresse;
But moral vertu, grounded upon trouthe,
That was the cause I first hadde on yow routhe.

(IV. 1667–73)

Though it elides Criseyde's actual physical response to his manly figure, this is not inconsistent with her thoughts in Book II, centring as they did on his deep commitment to her. More strikingly, even stunningly, it is a potent prediction of the central values of the novel, that 'moral virtue' that was made a totem in the criticism of the classic novel and that Austen, Dickens and Eliot made the core of their valued characters. Criseyde, it is clear, is not only a credible, capable and admirable woman: she is also, by being those things, a medium through which the voice can be heard which finds 'aray', 'noblesse' and all those listed public values to have a secondary status, and which finds an inner human power to be more real and more valuable.

Book V begins without a formal proem; narrative now sweeps on to continue, again like a novel, the action which ended Book IV.

Troilus was then not so much an external character as a hollowed shell (IV. 1699– 1701). Leaving their shared privacy, stripped of any inner dynamism, Troilus reverts in lifeless, automatic manner to something that seems like the baronial figure of Book I. He escorts Criseyde out of Troy:

> This Troilus, in wise of curteisye,
> With hauk on honde, and with an huge route
> Of knyghtes, rood and did hire companye,
>
> (V. 64–6)

But this and his whole life now is only 'in wise of curteysye,' a simulacrum of public activity. To encourage him, Pandarus urges they should go into society, and so, automatically accepting that social pressure, Troilus goes to Sarpedoun's house, a palace of comfort, company, and, in theory, consolation. But it is only misery to him; just as he formerly could only plan abduction of Criseyde, here he is quite separated from the public mode in which his position places him:

> For evere in oon his herte pietous
> Ful bisyly Criseyde, his lady, soughte.
>
> (V. 451–2)

The word 'sorwe' chimes through the text here and so do images of reversal: Troilus is like the figure of the Man in Black, but he was self-excluded from a vivid social world and showed by his language that he could rejoin it. Troilus is much more deeply mired in dysfunction. Failing to enjoy Sarpedoun's palace, he goes to Criseyde's — a substition which is one of the results of Chaucer's social elevation of the heroine. Troilus is confronted by this equally empty shell and calls it

> O thow lanterne of which queynt is the light
>
> (V. 543)

Gordon has written on this passage as the conclusion and summary of her book on ambiguity and irony in the poem,[42] and it brings to a head the patterns of social conflict described here. The external world is now valued only as a setting for its private human enclosures — the house is also called 'O ryng, fro which the ruby is out falle' (V. 549). And Troilus, left alone in what has become a lonely public world, is quite at a loss.

But the passage has another and darker implication. The word 'queynt' in that particular syntactic construction is ambiguous: Chaucer evidently knew quite well its second meaning as a taboo term for the vagina (see the Miller's tale, 3275–6); Troilus says that the light of the house is quenched, but his language also says that he got to this state by being obsessed with sex. This is one of the ironies identified with relish by the hard-line Christian interpretation, a series seen to culminate in the 'epilogue' to the whole poem. But this double meaning bears another message: that just as Troilus's deployment of love language in Book I was ineffective, fragments of a collectivity he did not share, so here his language has a slippery basis, he is so lost that even his own heartfelt statements have another and contradictory meaning in terms of common public parlance. His own behaviour becomes less and less sustainable in any rational terms as he waits for Criseyde, convincing himself that she is coming time after time when his expectation has once more failed. Socially marginal as he has become, he stands at the gate of the city, hoping for a happy re-entry not into its social life but his private communion with Criseyde: it is a striking image of his position, especially as written by a man who actually lived over one of the city gates and made the gates of Troy follow the practices of medieval London.

Criseyde was always suspicious of public forces and yet never completely overawed by them; lacking Troilus's commitment from birth to public life she felt able to operate within its interstices. In her new context in the Greek camp she shows herself, in her grief at the loss of her private communion, nevertheless capable of at first stimulating, then accepting and finally living a new life as Diomede's partner. When he first approaches her, even as they ride away from Troy, she hardly hears him in her own near-dysfunction. But nevertheless she contrives to maintain the social contact that her dangerous state and fearful character demand:

> But natheles she thonked Diomede
> Of al his travaile and his goode cheere,
> And that hym list his frendshipe hiro to bede;
> And she accepteth it in good manere,
> And wol do fayn that is hym lief and dere,
> And trusten hym she wolde, and wel she myghte,
> As seyde she; and from hire hors sh'alighte.
>
> (V. 183–9)

Her journey is over, she has a new world to live in, she at least practises the modes of social intercourse and setting up a new web of social dependence, with her own contribution taking the form of politeness and promised fidelity. The fact that Diomede is a distinctly rapacious practitioner of selfish pleasure within the mask of public values, a Pandarus-like figure who manipulates only for himself, naturally disrupts her simple expectations, and she is pressed by him steadily to grant a fuller friendship and finally the rewards of a lover — much as she was on Troilus's behalf, though not by him. But this new liaison is never a private relationship and is never presented in the detailed internal mode that Book II introduced and Book III brought to fulfilment. After Diomede presents himself as a suffering lover in the formal mode, she

> Graunted, on the morwe, at his requeste,
> For to speken with hym at the leeste,
>
> (V. 949–50)

And then his pressure and her isolation draw her further into what the narrator has called, with sharp evaluation, Diomede's 'net' (V. 775):

> Retornyng in hire soule ay up and down
> The wordes of this sodeyn Diomede,
> His grete estat, and perel of the town,
> And that she was allone and hadde nede
> Of frendes help; and thus bygan to brede
> The cause whi, the sothe for to telle,
> That she took fully purpos for to dwelle.
>
> (V. 1023–9)

This insightful narrative, the mode of Criseyde's personality before, does not lead her to love him; she only accepts him as a part of her enforced socialization and she follows its behavioural modes with a conscious separation from internally felt behaviour: 'To Diomede algate I wol be trewe' (V. 1071). This relationship is not the stunning transaction of personal and physical love that she and Troilus shared; rather it is the complex of social pressures that led medieval women to marry where they felt they must, to make a contract for want of a better option, and then to set themselves to keep its terms. Chaucer presents this as the basis for Criseyde's much discussed 'treachery', and that is why the narrator intervenes to conceal the time she took to 'betray' Troilus and to say 'I wolde excuse hire yit for routhe' (V. 1099). This statement is based not on his personal feeling for Criseyde as an over-individualist response has felt,[43] not on some vague sympathy with the lot of women, and especially not on the automatic criticism of Criseyde transmitted in the public tradition. The statement stems from a fully understood and brilliantly realized understanding of how and why people make decisions that go against their inner wishes and feelings.

So Criseyde is returned to a world of social life, however negative it seems and although the traces of her modal individuation remain to explain the transition. A remarkable and polemical formal device is used to mark this movement away from the private world. Late in the poem, deep in the turbulence of Book V, comes a formal set of descriptions of the three major characters, Diomede, Criseyde and Troilus (V. 799–840). Readers and critics have often felt this to be disruptive, a stray piece of medieval convention disturbing the surface of this near-novel. Disruption is often a sign of strain within the text, and this is a classic example. The formal statement marks the containment of the text's adventurous private modality. Diomede is presented briefly but publicly as a typical man of war 'Hardy, testif, strong and chivalrous' (V. 802). Troilus is outlined admiringly in fully conventional and idealistic terms as a princely knight:

> Yong, fressh, strong, and hardy as lyoun;
> Trewe as stiel in ech condicioun.
>
> (V. 830–1)

Between the two, as the narrative has placed her, stands Criseyde with her 'riche beaute', than whom there is 'no fairer creature', to be dealt with in the highest terms of idealism — 'Paradis stood formed in her eyen' (V. 808, 817– 8). But two touches remind the reader of her special status as a person who lives inwardly and has stimulated the poem's adventure towards an internalized literary presentation. She is now no more than 'mene' of 'stature', when at first she was said to be more than small (V. 806 and I. 281). And though the formal embrace of literary convention has shrunken her impact, there is one touch of her electric uniqueness: 'hire browes joyneden yfere' (V. 813). While the text accepts and creates in its patterns the fact that in a world still primarily public the private life cannot sustain itself, there is still a vestige at least of the inner and individual world that has been glimpsed and lost.

Pandarus is absent from these portraits, and he has faded from the text, partly because he is in technical terms a functionary like the narrator in *The Book of the Duchess*, but also for evaluative reasons. This man has manipulated so much, has been very active and voluble in deploying the pressures of the world upon the instincts and fears of the individuals he manipulates, but in his last appearance he is without voice or motion: in the face of 'his frendes sorwe' and what his niece has done he

> . . . stant, astoned of thise causes tweye,
> As still as ston; a word ne kowde he saye.

> (V. 1728–9)

It is a fine judgement on this volatile friend of Troilus, this irresponsible uncle of Criseyde, who pitched the one ill-prepared into a life he could not handle and persuaded the other to release powers that her surroundings prevented her from sustaining: he is ultimately the only one who is truly and permanently dysfunctional.

Troilus, distraught as he is, nevertheless returns to his former public life-style, and the language of the poetry accordingly changes to an epic mode — the recurrence of the epic frame — as the poet presents Troilus's new military mode (V. 1751–4), and admits he could have written in Vergilian style (V. 1766). But he made a different decision, and chose the topic of love (V. 1768–9). This self-conscious moment introduces the *envoi* to the poem, and it is a striking sequence of statements. The author's apology to women for not speaking conventionally of Criseyde's guilt (V. 1772– 85), the sending of his 'litel bok' into the company of great writers of the past (V. 1786–92), the sense that he might write differently and less disturbingly on another occasion (V. 1793–9) — those statements all cohere into a sense of the special character of what has here been produced. Not a fully conventional mediation of public wisdom to be sent into the world of cultural fame like a message from the 'House of Rumour', the book, its words and its topic are more particular than that: they have their own inner validity and status, albeit a disturbing and even fragile one. The power to realize in form the private mode of life that has been evident but also contained by more public modes throughout the poem — that is the stimulus for those striking statements.

They stand not at the end of the poem, but at the end of its authentic development of its argument about a public world and private possibilities. There follows what some critics call the 'epilogue', especially if they feel it is contrary to the drift of the poem — as Curry and Aers have thought, two critics most sensitive to medieval realities.[44] Others who feel that the Christian rejection of worldly affairs is current throughout the text have not liked the term 'epilogue' at all, but have felt this is the 'vertical' text of the poem, analogous to *The Book of the Duchess*'s opening statement about nature and sorrow.

This ending provides a further sublimation of Troilus within a public mode that is believed to be more lasting than Trojan or medieval feudalism. Touching in an epic nuance with the opening words 'The wrath', just as the Iliad opens, (V. 1800) the text nevertheless dispenses with epic feelings and raises Troilus to some pre-Christ version of the Christian heaven, from which he laughs at those who weep for him. And so, the poem fluently instructs all people:

> Repeyreth hom fro worldly vanyte,
> And of youre herte up casteth the visage
> To thilke God that after his ymage
> Yow made, and thynketh al nys but a faire
> This world, that passeth soone as floures faire.
>
> (V. 1837–41)

This rejection of the world dallies in the rhyme almost lovingly on worldly language — 'visage', 'image' and 'faire' in two senses. A more austere type of rejection is called up in rather stiff rhetorical formality, dismissing in the compulsive rhetorical form of *repetitio* the Trojan furniture of the poem: 'payens corsed olde rites' and 'all hire goddes', also its human and passionate 'wrecched worldes appetites' and even the mode of communication that has detained and delighted the audience for so long: 'the forme of olde clerkis speche In poetrie' (V. 1849–55).

Gower and Strode, Chaucer's own stern-minded friends, are invoked as if to strengthen his hand in this radical rejection of his own achievement, and the last stanza, fluently liturgical, presents a figure capable of providing consolation in such a holocaust of temporal pleasures and values, Christ himself. An authority is finally found, as it was not in either *The Book of Fame* or *The Parliament of Fowls*, and yet it is very much a last-minute, last-stanza discovery. Till then the text has only contained itself in a disturbed and unconvincing way, much as *The Canterbury Tales* will do.

The containment of this most radical piece of literary sociology continued outside its own textual limits, for Chaucer himself stated that the later *Legend of Good Women* was written to apologize for the affront done to the state of women by realizing Criseyde in the startlingly understanding way of this text. The God of Love, that idealized figure of power, said sternly to him in *The Legend*:

> Has thow nat mad in Englysh ek the bok
> How that Crisseyde Troylus forsok
> In shewynge how that wemen han don mis?
> But natheless, answere me now to this,
> Why noldest thow as wel han seyd goodnesse
> Of wemen, as thow hast seyd wikednesse?
>
> (G prologue, 264–9)

But only from the standpoint of conservative and collective assumptions can Chaucer be accused of speaking about Criseyde's 'wikednesse': the charge itself dismisses his own adventure, which was actually a greater threat to feudal stasis. The prologue, that is, provides questions that should only generate fully conservative and medieval answers: a classic example of an ideological problematic at work. But such constraints can have dialectic reflexes: Chaucer does not entirely do what his prologue demands. Just as he refined it towards a non-medieval, non-Gothic structure in the revised G version, so he also included a coded restatement of his radical revisionary purpose in *Troilus and Criseyde*, partly by including figures like Medea and Cleopatra under the bland title 'Good Women' and partly by inserting a whole set of ironies which some have taken to be half-concealed mockery of love or sniping at women, but which are more accurately interpreted as unsettling comments that undermine the confidence of the imposed collective form and suggest that the whole matter can be seen in another light — a view approached if not adopted by Frank.[45]

Williams suggested in a generally scorned piece of historicism that Chaucer based *Troilus and Criseyde* on the relationship between the Duke of Lancaster and his own sister-in-law Katharine Swynford.[46] That is both reductive and unproveable. But it comes closer to the real drive of the poem than all the devout readings of it as a general and ideal statement of timeless verities, Christian or humanist. The poem does bear in on fourteenth century human relations and realize, in tremendous detail and with extraordinary feeling, the experience not of one couple but of people, at a time when the collective patterns of social structure, behaviour and feeling were in a process of radical changes, a change capable of being fully traced to its sources in the economic and social structures of late medieval Britain. It is no accident that the other finished masterpiece of poetic art in the period, *Sir Gawain and the Green Knight*, makes its hero experience with pain and dismay the gap opening between honorific confidence and internalized values. What had always been an inner strain of romance, the inherent conflict between competitive assertiveness and honourable collectivity, was in this period becoming a major fissure along which imaginative artists were able to trace the patterns of social change in their community.

The dynamic of *Troilus and Criseyde*, that makes sharp-edged and vivid over centuries its patterns of art, is the unique fidelity with which it realizes, through the medium of love and focusing on the viewpoint of Criseyde herself, the strains and disorientation suffered by people as the social and cultural patterns of modern consciousness were beginning to exist. The scope of narrative and theme of *Troilus and Criseyde* is narrow, but tremendously deep. In *The Canterbury Tales* Chaucer would broaden his range in terms of social variety, literary types and contemporary conflicts. But the sheer intensity of the historical imagination in *Troilus and Criseyde* remains unique in Chaucer's work and with few parallels in English or any other literature.

3 *The Canterbury Tales*

I Preface

Chaucer's *Canterbury Tales* was his most popular work. There are reckoned to be eighty-five surviving manuscripts which contain the poem or at least a part of it — sometimes as little as a few surviving pages, or merely one or two selected tales. Fifty-five reasonably complete versions of the *Tales* still exist in manuscript;[1] many of them differ radically in tale-order, content and detailed text from the standard *Canterbury Tales* found in the best-known modern editions. The early printed versions repeat some of those patterns, and also introduce their own variations. These many versions of *The Canterbury Tales* can be seen, in the light of reception theory and ideological analysis, not as mere footnotes to some modern and supremely authorized edition of the poem, but as the continuous sociocultural re-creation of a poem whose inherent vigour has lent dynamism to all those different versions.

This book too has its own version, its own function in place and time, as a re-historicizing of *The Canterbury Tales*, both in terms of its own period and of history since then, especially the present. The underlying premise, as mentioned above (p. 2), is that literature is not 'related to' society, not a foreground against which society and history are background, but that the cultural production is itself a social act, interpreting, processing, analyzing, obscuring — even conditioning and shaping — other parts of social reality. So the following discussion does not start with a context and then place the tales against it. Rather, as in the previous chapter, there follows a detailed historically conscious discussion of the tales which reveals that they are themselves deeply aware of the social history of human confrontation with complex forces, a realization of what Raymond Williams has called a period's 'structure of feeling'.[2]

However, one area of discussion is most usefully made outside the detailed analysis of the poem, and made before that begins. This is the interaction between the text and the major socio-historical event of its period, the Peasants' Revolt of 1381. It has been usual in Chaucer criticism to say that whereas his contemporaries Langland and Gower make clear responses to the revolt (in Langland's case general but quite deep, in Gower's specific and rather shallow), Chaucer only makes a passing reference, late in the Nun's Priest's tale — some add a stanza in the Clerk's tale as a possible reference to mob politics (see pp. 144 and 111 for details).

The fact of the matter is that most commentators have not themselves been very interested in the Peasants' Revolt, nor very conscious of the way in which fictional artists deal with contemporary material. Critics who see Langland and Gower as more socially attuned than Chaucer miss a crucial difference of genre between them. Langland and Gower are writing allegory, the mode consistently used in medieval (and much classical) literature for research and analysis into society, both worldly and heavenly. Chaucer's three dream visions are themselves good examples of such an approach, as the first section of this book has shown. Chaucer came late to narrative because English medieval stories would have seemed naïve, not composed for people of deep learning (they read Latin) or courtly sophistication (they understood French). An ambitious court poet would naturally have turned first to French models, which were non-narrative; it was only through encountering the complex narratives of Boccaccio that Chaucer appreciated the power of fiction to realize forces and themes of complex and contemporary character. In potent fictional narratives, these forces and themes are consistently displaced from the conscious foreground and realized through the mediation of human experience, as structures of feeling. Jane Austen does deal powerfully with the position of women, but does so experientially, for example through Elizabeth Bennett's despair at her friend Charlotte's wretched life. Dickens in the same way does confront industrial capitalism, but it is, as in

Dombey and Son or *Our Mutual Friend*, dramatized through its human impact and social relations.

Chaucer treats the social forces of his own period by creating them in these human and experiential terms. The detail of this process will be set out through this chapter. At times the poem approaches explicit references to the class conflict that grew to a head in the Peasants' Revolt itself, as has been noticed in a limited way by some recent critics.[3] But there is also a general overriding interaction between the poem and the revolt, which has gone unnoticed because specific history is so rarely enmeshed with a treatment of the text.

The revolt was centred on London and the surrounding areas. Essex was a major scene of unrest but the most revolutionary part was Kent, where the rising centred on Maidstone and, in particular, Canterbury. On 10th June, 1381, within days of the first movements, a large band probably led by Wat Tyler marched on Canterbury. What Oman called 'the capture of Canterbury' occurred when the revolutionaries entered the Cathedral in search of Archbishop Sudbury, destroyed legal records through the town and insisted that the people support the 'true commons' and the King.[4] There was apparently little physical assault and no murder. Next day this remarkably well-disciplined army marched on London. They arrived on Black-heath on 12th June, just where the highway still arrives from Canterbury. They were in Southwark that evening opening the jail, and at Mile End by the next morning. This was the major single thrust of the revolt into the capital and against the establishment.

Chaucer certainly knew about this dramatic climax — the murder of Sudbury and the sacking of John of Gaunt's Savoy palace were notorious, and his own apartments over Aldgate faced Mile End: the rebels entered London literally under his eyes. Furthermore, his links with Kent are a good deal stronger and earlier than are generally recognised: later he was JP and MP in the county, but his own family had Kent connections, he had already held wardships near Canterbury and his close friend Sir Richard Sturry no doubt had connections with the small town of that name next to Canterbury.[5]

Chaucer's personal knowledge and undoubtedly alarmed interest in the march from Canterbury to London should not seem to contradict his apparent reticence about the revolt; his knowledge is, in fact, central to the overarching ideology of the plan of the tales themselves. The route of the pilgrims from Southwark to Canterbury is the exact reverse of that taken by the revolutionaries, and, as will be shown in detail below, the issues raised in the frame-story and within the tales often deal with problems raised in the revolt and its aftermath.

The world of *The Canterbury Tales* is the world of conflict that generated the Peasants' Revolt, and one of the major forces of the long poem is to realize the unrest and the quest for freedom and individual rights that were all central to this historically potent period. They were not presented with approval: Chaucer's own social position does not suggest he would sympathize with revolution, and frequently there are signs that the forces of conflict are realized under strain and arouse inevitable constraint. Ultimately those forces are neutralized in a number of ways. One of them is the overall plan, that contemporary conflict is being recreated within the model of a pilgrimage which is both a physical reversal of the peasants' march and also a cultural reversal of their secular and political concerns into an eventually dominant spiritual mode.

Uniquely powerful as that idea was in Chaucer's hands, it was not unique. Both Boccaccio and Sercambi (possible sources, or at least analogues, for the story-collection idea) had used pilgrimage as a structure to escape in culture something dreadful – the plague in their cases. And contemporary writings do set in opposition pilgrimage to Canterbury and the revolt that surged from there to London. The chronicles record several encounters between violent peasants and holy pilgims – one of them no less than Joan, wife of the Black Prince and now queen mother. Froissart has a story that not even Oman believes about King Richard's visit to Ospringe to mete out justice to revolutionaries: that was the last overnight stop before Canterbury, and the king's vengeful mission mimics pilgrimage in a way unmissable in the period.[6]

So the journey itself and its reversal of revolt into pilgrimage in a major overarching pattern of the text, especially in its final form where the pilgrims are never shown returning to London and telling tales on the way back, as was planned: the whole plot is subsumed into a religious and conservative conclusion.

Another structure within the poem, more detailed and more far-reaching, becomes clear when the tales are read in terms of their sociohistorical force. Three major sequences exist in *The Canterbury Tales*, which are in part co-terminous with the manuscript fragments as they are constructed and ordered in what can reliably be received as the best order, the one which is most strongly attested and also has the most powerful impact.[7]

The first sequence runs from the general prologue to the end of the Man of Law's tale; its dominant issue is the observation of social conflict, an initial mapping of the forces of the late fourteenth century English world. This is followed by the second sequence, which contains many famous tales and runs from the Wife of Bath's prologue right through to the end of the Pardoner's tale. This is not merely the 'marriage group' extended; as will be argued below, this builds on the first sequence by consistently projecting the historical imagination from the position of particular pilgrims, not in terms of their 'personalities' as humanist criticism has limited the text, but in terms of the social potential of the forces symbolized by each pilgrim.

The third and final sequence withdraws from both the poetic power and the analytic daring of the great second sequence. At first, from Shipman's tale to the end of the Nun's Priest's tale, it is a single manuscript fragment, well-finished but limited — limited, that is, in terms of Chaucer's possibilities, however potent it might seem in comparison with other writers of the period. These tales merely fill out the ideas of the general prologue; they represent genres in thorough but not adventurous fulfilment and conclude with the negative brilliance of the Nun's Priest. Chaucer's own contribution in the third sequence rejects poetry itself for a prosaic and moral statement of conservatism. That position is fully developed in the last four tales; they firmly reject secular skills and values, offering as a positive the full force of the Christian religion.

But the power of the whole text's realization of contemporary forces, human and political, is such that even the steadily Christian and conservative end to the *Canterbury Tales* itself shows distinct signs of strain in its efforts to contain what has gone before, that dynamic creation of the experience of late fourteenth century life which gives *The Canterbury Tales* its veracity, at once historical and imaginative.

II From the general prologue to the Man of Law's tale: 'Diverse folk diversely they seyde'

The structure of *The Canterbury Tales* is usually called a 'frame story', a fiction which explains why all these tales are being told. Boccaccio's *Decameron* and Sercambi's *Novelle*, both written before the *Tales*, also have stories told before a group of people on a pilgrimage, though Sercambi's narrator tells them all. Chaucer's frame story, however, has two special features, both of which mesh powerfully with the historical dynamism of the Tales.

Chaucer stresses mobility much more than Boccaccio, who keeps his people in one place all the time, and more than Sercambi who does make his characters wander, but the stories are always told at night when they have stopped. Both patterns are in fact much more realistic than Chaucer's fantasy of tales told on the move: his image of a mobile, listening, responding group is much closer to the fantastic 'House of Rumour' than has been recognized. Mobility, both social and geographic, is a key motif in the tales, just as it was in the rapidly and visibly changing socioeconomic structure of the period.

The other striking feature of Chaucer's structure is that the frame story begins to grow in relation to the tales themselves. Boccaccio makes some movement towards an appropriate narrator — the same figure tells the 'obscene' stories, for example. But some at least of Chaucer's narrators grow into much more than a peg for a story. Figures like Pardoner, Wife of Bath and Franklin are presented vividly in the general prologue and their tales have some aspects of a speech in character. That movement towards individuation is, like mobility, itself a part of the changing experience of life in the late fourteenth century. It was visible both in economic terms, as people could earn and save and invest and make private profit, and also in cultural terms, especially in religion as Christian values were, through Lollardry, mysticism and what became called *devotio moderna*, pressing towards a private relationship with God. The depth of Chaucer's historical imagination and the formal ways in which it can operate are clearly revealed by this structural realization of mobility and individuation.

The opening lines of the general prologue are arresting, memorable and subtly elusive. They state vividly the rhythms of nature and then insist that people naturally desire to go on pilgrimage:

> And specially from every shires ende
> Of Engelond to Caunterbury they wende,
> The hooly blisful martir for to seke,
> That hem hath holpen whan that they were seeke.
>
> (15–18)

This opening elides what most of the poem will be about, the natural and secular life of people; there is a striking absence between animal vitality and human religiousness. But before this elegant omission of the conflicted social world is ultimately ratified in the religious end of the *Tales*, a whole set of forces are drawn into that vacuum, a world of social and historical conflict among the 'sondry folk' who come together in 'felaweshipe' (25–26); they are the medium for Chaucer's imaginative dramatization of the dynamic forces of his period.

A Knight comes first. The indefinite article is usually ignored: commentators usually say '*The* Knight comes first.' But these pilgrims are rarely given the singular definition of that article. Medieval readers understood the basis of personality in the general prologue. Many manuscripts have marginal notes to indicate where each description begins. They either say 'A Knight,' 'A Prioress', 'A Clerk' and so on, or just 'Knight', 'Prioress', 'Clerk'. The pilgrims are basically archetypal, not individual, however much some may be developed towards individuation. Recognizing that he is *a* knight, it is easier to tackle another misunderstood matter, the order of the general prologue. It has been quite usual to call it haphazard but there are some ordering principles. Brooks observed sensibly that the whole sequence, from Knight to Pardoner, goes from social high and good to anti-socially low and vile, though he was not clear about the order in between.[8] Similarly, there are obvious elements of order in the Knight's 'family' and the set of regular religious figures, Prioress, Monk and Friar; Chaucer himself points to the 'churls' grouping from the Miller on (542–4). But these fragments of order do not give an overall plan.

Many commentators have noted the presence of three figures typifying the medieval idea of social structure: the three estates of landholders, landworkers and spiritual workers are represented by Knight, Plowman and Parson. Their ideal character, both in terms of value and of descriptive technique, has seemed to some to provide an evaluative core against which the self-seeking and physically depicted figures are set.[9] But this is not a dramatic order as such, and Mann, who knows the estates material best, feels strongly that it is not the model. Indeed, although the historical matrix of the poem is not her topic, she senses that there lies the answer: 'It is possible that social actualities affected the order which Chaucer developed for the prologue'.[10] Once the connection is seen and pursued, the order appears both lucid and powerful as an analytic realization of the contemporary world.

There are four different socially functional groups, the last one of which can be divided into three sections. They are:

1 The manorial family: Knight, Squire, Yeoman
2 The regular religious: Prioress, Monk, Friar
3 Professionals (people who depend for a living on skill, not on manorial tenure, religious vocation or on any form of service): Merchant, Clerk, Sergeant of Law, Franklin, Guildsmen and Cook, Shipman, Doctor, Wife of Bath.
4 Lower Classes: people who in one way or another serve others. These divide into:
    (a) Role-fulfilling servitors: Parson and Plowman
    (b) Role-abusing servitors: secular: Miller, Manciple, Reeve; religious: Summoner, Pardoner

This scheme shows that, unlike traditional estates satire, Chaucer had a clear view of a non-traditional social grouping which embraced scholars and merchants, lawyers, sea captains and women, so long as they had a money-making skill — this wife is an expert weaver, though she is introduced as if her craft were 'wiving', an equivocation to be developed in her prologue and tale.

Each of these groups is ranked internally in order of status (as are the sub-groups of group four). The order in group one is obvious; that in group two is straightforward since a Prioress outranks through her authority a simple monk and their houses long ante-date the mendicants, quite apart from their superior reputation in the period. In group four the Parson is evidently socially superior to his labouring brother (the Parson cannot be free-born because of this relationship) and the rest of the characters appear to be ordered by their increasing viciousness. A similar pattern appears in the 'Professionals' group. A merchant prince heads it both in wealth and in rationale — Howard suggested shrewdly that he leads to typify 'the mercantile basis for the "rise" of this social group'.[11] The rest follow in steadily diminishing status — an admired scholar, a slightly deceptive lawyer, a sensually obsessed Franklin. Five Guildsmen form a party that is the urban equivalent of the manor (a relationship noted by Marx[12]): their wives and their travelling servant are related to them, not to this group of pilgrims as a whole. Shipman and Doctor are distinctly doubtful in their practices, and the weaver-cum-wife's position here is both final and marginal, but she is a skilled and free person, not a servant or employee,[13] and she belongs with the other members of the newly free, mobile and disruptive forces who were remaking society and its economic structure at the same time. This had been going on for centuries, but in the fourteenth century social and economic change was so rapid, partly at least because of the plague, that it was evident and disturbing.[14] Chaucer was not alone in perceiving the changes in process, but this 'professional' group indicates how advanced was his analysis and understanding.

The prologue begins with the old world. The description of a knight insists he has done the knightly things, fighting overseas in wars, landings, tournaments, and always winning honour — that central value of the feudal and chivalric class. It was usually called 'worship' in English, and the concept lies behind the stress on 'worth' and 'worthy' (47, 50, 64, 68). In essence, chivalry was the ideological self-projection of cavalry. The men who dominated early medieval Europe were heavy cavalry, rapacious, cruel and acquisitive — French as well as Norman. The chivalric notion of behaving nobly to each other and to ladies was a behavioural ideal to mask their real violence and to dignify themselves. Romance itself was a genre created to realize this pattern.[15]

In a vigorous book presenting Chaucer's Knight as a deeply ironic portrait, Terry Jones shows how contemporary reality differed from chivalric ideology, but that does not mean that this Knight is in reality 'a new style mercenary'.[16] That is a humanist misreading, too concerned with *the* Knight: here, at least, Chaucer's art is less personalized. The ideal of knighthood is offered, with the disturbing reality distantly visible; the Knight's tale will show that ideal, in the face of reality, to be no more than an ineffective and doomed ideology.

The Knight's son, a squire, is an archetype of amatory chivalry, that complex structure called in the medieval period *fin amor* and later on courtly love.[17] The Squire's description is a series of motifs from the *fin amor* world, showing military prowess and courtesy as being the crucial practices for the young knight who hopes to ascend in terms of honour, that is in property and power.[18] But now, though 'Curteis', he knows his currently 'lowely' place (99) in the hierarchy of military landholders. Both his tale and his father's will explore further the fantasies and realities of courtesy and *fin amor*.

Another manorial figure is a Yeoman, who fulfils the double role of supporting his lord in war and tending his forests during peace. In both functions, what seems an amiable member of the rank and file, at once neat and strong, was in reality a formidable source of profit and power for his master. When Chaucer wrote, the British bowmen had already twice cut down the French cavalry at Crecy and Poitiers, bringing wealth and territorial power to the crown and its supporters, aristocratic and professional. At home the Yeoman defends the forest and its animals for the lord's pleasure and profit, against bondmen trying to augment their food — his role was bitterly resented over the centuries.

So the manorial family displays a series of social and ideological stereotypes in action. The regular religious group, however, opens with role reversal. Smiling and courtly oaths are noticed in this Prioress, not the expected serious demeanour or oaths of chastity, poverty and stability. The language heard is not the Latin of her proper services, but colloquial and secular French. Her name focuses the matter: Madame Eglantyne is a sweetly pretty name, but distinctly unreligious for an important nun.

This idea of a pleasant woman rather than a weighty nun is pursued through her table manners and love of animals, and develops a cutting edge. The description sets itself 'for to speken of hir conscience' (142); it starts 'She was so charitable and so pitous' (143). Major Christian concepts lie behind conscience (the voice of God in humans), charity (love) and pity (mercy), but in her they are demeaned to no more than a sentimental attachment to animals. This is in part a realistic picture of a contemporary gentlewoman penned in an unsuitable nunnery, as happened to many women who missed or avoided marriage in the period, and at the same time it illustrates the spiritual impoverishment possible in the contemporary church.

The Monk's description follows the pattern of the Prioress's. Words like 'maistrie', 'outridere', 'venerie', 'manly' (165–7) at once imply he breaches monastic chastity: in the following and focusing image it is his bridle bell that is heard, not the service bell of his abbey. Like the Prioress, his figure has a sleek, engaging physicality that defines his own concerns. In him the personal voice suggested in the Prioress's French is developed and actually heard: at 177–82 and 187–8 the narrator quotes his rejection of the historical and central role of monastic life.

Greed, worldliness, a personal voice, sensuality to the point of sexual indulgence: these motifs are made central to the description of a Friar, a long and notably fluent vignette rich in polysyllabic and French-sounding rhyme words that memorably mimic the Friar's fluent and manipulative tongue, as in 220–4 and 244–8.

The mendicant orders were founded to combat by persuasion and a living model the licence and heresy that St Francis and St Dominic saw in the church: to speak of one of their followers as 'wantowne and merye' (208) indicates how far the ideal had fallen. Full of skill and charm, this Friar uses it for his own ends, more disruptive and harmful than the self-indulgence of Prioress and Monk. When he is 'Curteis' and 'lowely of servyse' (250) this is not, as in the Squire, a deferral to authority. Chaucer may have taken the corruption of a friar less seriously — or less centrally — than did Langland, but he is aware of the social threat posed by the friars, and this pilgrim continues that analysis.

It is an easy transition from the mercantile Friar to a Merchant, but these two groups, regular religious and professionals, are separate, and there is in function a great difference between the two: the Merchant is no peddler like the Friar, nor a shopkeeper, as the title of merchant is now understood. He is a merchant prince, overseeing trade ventures, investing thoughtfully and dealing primarily in medieval offshore banking, moving money around the world for maximum profit. The Merchant is an early capitalist, making his stock of capital generate profit, whether by investment and sale or by money manipulation itself.

This brief and generalized portrait stresses lofty concerns and

internal emptiness: "Ther wiste no wight that he was in dette'
(280) is followed by showy language that conceals bankruptcy,
real and moral:

So estatly was he of his governaunce
With his bargaynes and with his chevyssaunce.

(281–2)

The idea of a hollow mercantile rhetoric is to be brilliantly
developed in the Merchant's tale; the prince is only a merchant,
after all.

A Clerk who follows seems not to be criticized: he is given only
to greed for books and nothing suggests that to be bad or even
unworldly. He has no personal voice, no love of money or display;
he does not stand out against ideal role-fulfilment. Even the joke
about the 'philosopher's stone' turning base metal into gold (297–
8) is favourable, unlike its later treatment in the Canon's
Yeoman's tale. This Clerk belongs among the professionally
skilled individuals, not with the religious. He is part of the new
world of professional learning, like Chaucer's friend Strode,
apparently both a London lawyer and a leading Oxford
mathematician.

Sergant of the Law is, like Merchant, very rich, highly skilled
and distinctly a man of misleading surfaces: 'seeming' is stressed
(313 and 322) to suggest he lacks both inner honesty and some of
the success he claims. Lawyers were a prime target of the 1381
revolutionaries, and while this is a much less aggressive attitude
to them, it stresses both their importance and their doubtful value
as figures of a somewhat threatening new world.

A Franklin who accompanies the lawyer and has some legal
skill and function has been interpreted either as the last of the
aristocracy or as a part of the lower gentry moving upwards. The
most recent opinion is firmly that he is not quite in the top
drawer, for all his wealth.[19] Both the description and its location
in this group indicate that administrative skills have been central
to his present position, rather than inheritance, warfare, or any
other acquisition of power and property. This inherent individualism connects, as in the regular religious, with an extreme
interest in sensual comfort: a conspicuous display of nouns
loads down this passage with things possessed and implicitly
over-valued by this prosperous arriviste.

The five guildsmen are much more cursorily dealt with

perhaps because Chaucer euphemizes his own family's context. The emphasis on fine clothes, with knives for show and purses for use sketches effectively figures who are both parvenu and mercantile. They are a group, though, and like Knight and Prioress they have a follower in the Cook, as well as their wives. Also like the Knight they have property and income (373), but they live in an exchange economy, as their purses suggest, and their honour is not innate but anxiously defended — their wives are snobs (374–8). Their servant, unlike the Yeoman or the Prioress's followers, is only there for creature comforts. Just as Merchant and Lawyer were men of seeming, not of substance, the life style that is so important to the Guildsmen and the Franklin is inauthentic — the snowstorm of food in the Franklin's house (345) and the Cook's ulcer (386) both have a negative impact.

A Shipman would be the executive officer of a Merchant's schemes, without 'nyce conscience' (398); his brown face, plain dress and ordinary horse bring him into close and somewhat threatening focus. The name of his ship need not suggest a real man: it brings specificity to the scene, thickening further the sense that this group creates: a world of work, motion, conflict, conniving, even murder — business practices realized in lively and distasteful detail. The new world is comprehended and judged at once.

In the same vein is a Doctor, a man whose quantified knowledge and financial success is stressed much more than his healing art. The description is weighed down with medical authorities and medicines, and the malign relation of healing and profit is created as the narrator sarcastically gives the wrong reason for his interest in gold:

> For gold in phisik is a cordial,
> Therefore he lovede gold in special.

(443–4)

Each of these professionals has dealt with money; in the Clerk's case, rejecting it, though he still had a 'litel' in his 'cofre' (298). Skills, rewards, sensuality, self-seeking: these have been the dominant motifs in a group of figures for which there were no existent role-models to follow[20] and which Chaucer has masterfully and imaginatively made a social grouping, sharing features of behaviour just as they share a place in the emergent socioeconomic structure.

To them he adds the best known of his pilgrims, a Wife of Bath. A fully credible picture of a female weaver,[21] she combines the roles of the professional men and the burgess's wives. She has skills, vigour and self-interest, but she is also snobbish and concerned with display — as indeed are several of the men. But her independence is constructed primarily from an anxiously patriarchal viewpoint: her mobility is implicitly sexual ('She koude muchel of wandrynge by the weye' (467)) and so are her skills — 'Of remedies of love she knew per chaunce, For she koude of that art the olde daunce' (475–6). She is placed last because weaving is the least prestigious of the skills in this group, not necessarily because she is a woman; she is both the most marginal and the most complex of the figures, as is suggested by her lack of a professional title and by the way in which social and sexual matters interweave, both here and in her prologue and tale.

Against the wife's mobile and florid femininity, and the specific, money-ridden and privatized character of the professional group as a whole, the opening part of group four, the Parson and the Plowman, stands in severe and critical contrast. The lower orders at first replicate the pattern of groups one and two; they were concerned with the manor and the church, and these areas are now seen through the work of archetypal and humble role-fulfillers, with the church coming first; a parson takes precedence of his toiling brother.

Unlike the freeborn regular religious and their opening role-reversals, the Parson is immediately presented with a welter of words that locate the figure in the ideal mainstream of a working church: 'good', 'povre', 'riche . . . of hooly thoght and werk', 'lerned', 'trewely', 'devoutly', 'Benygne', 'wonder diligent', 'ful pacient' (476–84). Role-reversals are only mentioned negatively: he did not excommunicate those who could not pay tithes, he did not fail to visit his troubled parishioners whatever the circumstances, he never abandoned his people to seek a comfortable life in London. There is no physical detail at all, but that should not suggest that the description is flat. It is the longest of all and notably effective in oral performance, a smooth, flowing and persuasive statement of the ideal priest in specific action.

His brother is realized more briefly but equally ideally; not visualized at all, he is presented in terms of his busy and honest actions as he lived up to high standards 'in pees and parfit charitee' (532) — in every way he is the dutiful senior peasant, the ploughman's role in the community. There is an inherent politics here as Stilwell observed; the Plowman is a deliberately passive figure, designed to contain a different reality, 'a colorless figure for a good reason, namely that the real ploughman of the time was revolting against everything that Chaucer stood for'.[22]

Parson and ploughman together are rejections of the role that priests and skilled labourers played in the Peasants' Revolt. The importance of the two figures was indicated in 'John Ball's letter', the revolutionary rhyme which used the names of symbolic priest and ploughman:

> Johon Schep, some tyme Seynte Marie prest of York, and
> now of Colchestre, greteth wel Johan Nameles, and Johan
> the Millere, and John Cartere, and biddeth them that thei
> bee war of gyle in borugh, and stondeth togidre in Godes
> name, and biddeth Pers Ploughman go to his werk. . . [23]

But if the lower orders of the general prologue are at first symbolically ideal and peaceful, the disorderly possibilities of their social level are not ignored. Aware of their class character, the narrator sums them up in 542–4 and starts with a Miller. The similar linking of priest, ploughman and miller in the rhyme just quoted may be an accident. But millers were the senior working tenants of a lord and several men named Miller appear among the leaders of the peasants' revolt.[24]

This Miller is certainly a figure of physical force, with the strength typical of productive workers in a barely mechanized world — 'Ful byg he was of brawn, and eek of bones' (546) states his impact in a muscular tone. But this power is quickly and deftly sidetracked, first into destructive vigour, wrestling and door-smashing, and then into animality through images of pig and fox (552–6). The only mention of a skill is stealing, and it is cash-related as the 'thombe of gold' suggests (563).

A Manciple is the Miller's antitype — urban, non-physical, quiet — yet he is equally disruptive and self-seeking, as the description finally reveals. The lawyers he serves are fit to guide the landed lords (another statement of legal power in the period) but they are subverted by their cunning servitor (586). If the Miller's description showed physical power sidetracked and contained, the Manciple's suggests a more insidious way of inverting the hierarchical pyramid.

The Reeve, the manor's senior administrative official, is also finally revealed as working for his private interests, not the general good (609). Lean and arid, he is the Miller's opposite; his craft of carpentry is long past and he wields the weapons of the Manciple. His demeanour is that of a cleric (590, 621) not a rumbunctious peasant, and the opposition between Miller and Reeve, worker and administrator, which is to explode in their tales, is already underlined by the fact that while the physical Miller leads the whole pilgrimage, the Reeve rides carefully last.

The religious self-seeking servitors are a stage deeper in physical and moral decay. A Summoner is a writ-server and catchpoll for the bishop's court, which deals in moral abuses and failure to pay the church its dues. His face at once proclaims his monstrosity, aflame with the fires not of God's love (as cherubs traditionally were, 624) but with sexual disease. This anti-cherub has anti-learning, a few parroted phrases of Latin to awe simple folk and aid his disruption of the archdeacon's order for his own ends. The description reveals the inner subversion of church authority at the lowest and most public level.

A Pardoner is 'freend and his compeer' (670) to this Summoner, and they sing together in disturbing harmony. Where the Summoner is a corrupt and disruptive church policeman, the Pardoner is a bogus priest, with all the added power of that role. At first he is presented as physically disgusting yet vain and assertive — and evidently sexually unusual. The text is not particularly interested in just what the Pardoner was, eunuch or castrato or even trans-sexual. The point is that he appears unnatural — and that is not an attack on homosexuals, but a metaphor for the way in which the Pardoner's great skills are radically shifted away from the proper role of the preacher and indulgence-seller towards his own private gain. It is certainly a conservative view of a homosexual (or whatever he is), but not a neurotic or vengeful one.

From line 692 on the text insists on the sheer skills of this grotesque 'noble ecclesiaste' (708). His tale will bear out that promise, and he is depicted already as an anti-parson who eats into the funds available to the true church. This is just what friars did as well, and the financial obsession, the perverted skills, the preening individuality of these two figures shows their relation; more instances of that link will be seen later, both in their tales and during the Wife of Bath's prologue.

All of these five 'churls' invert their roles, whether they are administrative or technical services to the manor (Reeve and Miller), a similar role at a lawyer's inn (Manciple) or administrative and official functions within the church (Summoner and Pardoner). All of these roles could have been, and no doubt were, fulfilled at times as nobly as Parson and Plowman do their work. But the Peasants' Revolt in particular and the general state of society indicate that the traditional role-models and the cultural authority of lord and church were decreasingly able to awe the servitors of the feudal world, whether secular or religious, into their roles. Mobility, personal and social, was shaping people into behaviour that, from an old-fashioned point of view seemed as selfish and as revolutionary as that so vividly described by Chaucer in the case of these churls.

There only remain the Host and the author, two real people — it is now accepted as 'certain' that Harry Bailly of the Tabard in Southwark is a real man, not only a type.[25] He is a burgess and businessman (754) and so belongs basically with the professionals of group three for all his occasionally vulgar and churlish behaviour. As his position in the prologue is marginal, so in the headlinks he will play a double-role, partly a normative authority, partly a vulgar and self-interested figure of the new world.

And there is the undescribed pilgrim, 'myself'. Not the heroic author of a novel or the insightful sage of a modern poem, but a mediator who passes on to us what he has seen and heard. This role is not only a medieval predecessor to the authorial ideal of bourgeois individualism: it also enables the text to withdraw from the innovative forces it realizes. The first point made by this non-author is to apologize for his churls, for 'hir wordes and hir cheere' if they should seem offensive (725–8).

This is not merely a matter of obscene words or bad manners. Chaucer will shape positions which are disruptive in political terms, his text will be to some extent a battleground for the forces of the period, and neither he nor many of his audience would approve of some of those forces. But they are to be created fictionally, with more power and with more daring than modern critics often can — or want to — see. The importance of the apology is that those forces of disruption are nowhere more powerfully and more threateningly realized than in the consciously crafted opening sequence to this deeply historical poem, from general prologue to Cook's tale.

The Host, for all the democratic apparatus of a draw for order, has a conservative pattern in mind. He arranges for the Knight to start, just as did the prologue. And he later asks the Monk, the next senior man, to follow, but this, like a lot of hierarchical plans, goes wrong. After the Knight finishes, the *Tales* are beset with disruption and its place is all the more authentic because it has already been realized in the tale of the Knight himself.

'The Knight's tale' is how the first of the stories is usually known. But remembering the general prologue it might be best to think of it as 'a Knight's tale': it is not one knight's efforts to be impressive and wise, but rather an archetypal, romance-like presentation of the world from the viewpoint of cavalry through the mouthpiece of chivalry.

For a knight to begin the tales, just as he does the general prologue, seems in support of traditional hierarchy, and many critics see his story in that light — for example, the very influential Muscatine:

> The impressive, patterned edifice of the noble life, its dignity and richness, its regard for law and decorum, are all bulwarks against the ever threatening forces of chaos, and in constant collision with them. And the crowning nobility, as expressed by the poem, goes beyond a grasp of the forms of social and civil order, being and magnificence in any earthly sense, to a perception of the order beyond chaos.[26]

That represents the consensus on the tale, especially by scholars from the lush American campuses. But 1960s Britain provided a much darker reception of the tale, particularly of its ending, seeing Theseus as a political leader who was making the best of the ruins about him. His methods seemed to fall far short of Muscatine's 'crowning nobility', being no more than threadbare philosophy and pragmatic opportunism.[27]

Some other scholars linked the tale to its period, but the connections they saw were no more than reflections of contemporary events. The text is more powerfully historical than that. Chaucer instinctively understood the ideological features of chivalric culture and stressed them in this story, to create not merely the simple wish-fulfilment of the ruling classes (Muscatine's interpretation) but rather to expose their position and its lack of genuine authority.

Authority, both aristocratic and masculine, is a central feature of medieval romance;[28] that dual claim to power is ideologically stated as the tale opens. Theseus has conquered the Amazons, turned them into inactive wife and demure sister;[29] in the same mode he generously gives mercy to ruined and distressed ladies (952–64). Towards men he is unyielding, and Chaucer realizes this in one of his additions, the stark and dominating figure in Theseus' banner:

> The rede statue of Mars, with spere and targe,
> So shyneth in his white baner large,
> That alle the feeldes glyteren up and down;
>
> (975–7)

The bloody Theseus similarly dominates the battlefields, a general of cavalry not a prince of chivalry.

Against the power of king and baron, romance sets the humble state of the individual and honour-less knight, the hero who will rise to splendour and property through a series of formulaic proving deeds: that was the wish-fulfilment mechanism of romance for the landless knights who provided the core of its original audience.[30] Palamon and Arcite are worst-case examples of the knight who has hit bottom. They are taken for dead and have nowhere to go. But their noble blood, as usual in romance, saves them. As is equally normal, love is the mechanism which ennobles the warriors, pointing them towards a new prosperity, which they will also earn by their fighting prowess. But romance used a single hero and ideologized his aggressive nature by making him fight ogres, oppressors of ladies and only in incognito let him fight his brother knights, other property hunters. Chaucer's story, by having two lovers of one woman, makes conflict central and overt, creating much more sharply than usual 'competitive assertiveness', that inherent acquisitive aggression which was the real core of the medieval knight's quest for wealth and honour.[31]

The collective ideology of knightly fraternity is broken because of Emily, the object of desire, the symbol of competition. The heroes argue, then they assume separate aspects of the knight in his painful motion through war and love towards assured success. Arcite is consciously aggressive — 'Ech man for hymself,' he says (1182), and Palamon is as desperate as any hero in his unrequited love for the wealthy lady (1118–22).

The plot of the Knight's tale stresses more heavily than in most romances the isolated and competitive nature of the warrior's climb to power, wealth and so honour. Arcite is released and exiled, and this device permits the potent image of his return as a serving-man. Like Gareth as a kitchen-hand in Malory's Tale V, like Chrétien de Troyes' Yvain as the anonymous 'Knight with the Lion', the hero goes beneath his chivalric self-concept to gain or regain that status — and so he realizes the humiliations and labours that knights really had to go through to win lands and authority. When Palamon escapes from jail he represents another sort of figure without status, lurking just outside chivalrous society. It is in these unchivalric but historically real states that the twin heroes meet and exercise their 'competitive assertiveness', fighting like wild animals (1656 and 1699).

Resolution of these desperate positions comes in romance through two agencies, often interwoven: the generous authority of the king, rewarding the hero for power in war (usually demonstrated in tournaments), and the generous response of the propertied lady who loves him for his qualities — which definitely include his martial powers. Part Two of the Knight's tale ends by relieving the tension with a promise of this dual release. Theseus decrees there will be a tournament for Emily's hand (1845–69): so competition is socialized and turned from a desperate cavalry encounter into the heights of martial and amatory chivalry.

From here romance would take a clear course. A splendid tourney, a tremendous fight to a draw, some resolution based on a device — the lady would have a sister, equally wealthy, or one hero would withdraw from the contest to follow other knightly quests. The reality of competition would be obscured by the re-imposition of fraternal ideology, as between Yvain and Gauvain, Gareth and Gawain. Chaucer's model, however, will not be so easy to resolve: Parts Three and Four show the mechanisms of splendour, jousting and love in operation — and show them ultimately not working because they are, like the aristocratic life itself, based on conflict.

Theseus expresses his power through splendid works, as did medieval kings in Europe. Nor is the cultural authority of religion forgotten at Athens. three temples are set in the walls of the splendid, circular (Round Table-like) jousting theatre. In describing each temple at length Chaucer follows his sources, but as in the dream poems he uses allegorical description to establish social analysis. The temple of Venus is a grimmer and more disturbing version of the temple in *The Parliament of Fowls*; in it are malign figures from the *Roman de la Rose* such as Ydlenesse and Narcissus, and also those who through time have been destroyed by the negative associations of love. The very bases of aristocratic ideology are here at risk:

> Beautee, ne sleighte, strengthe ne hardynesse
> Ne may with Venus holde champartie.

(1948–9)

The temple of Mars is a central element in the unmasking of aristocratic life. The figure of the god is no longer merely awesome as it was in Theseus' banner, but austere, violent and, to use Chaucer's own poetically emphasized words, 'grisly' and 'gastly' (1971, 1984). This military power is the source of all kinds of human disasters, both the allegorical summaries of Felonye, Ire and Drede, and the vividly realized horrors of human conflict:

> The smylere with the knyf under the cloke;
> The shepne brennynge with the blake smoke;
> The tresoun of the mordrynge in the bedde;
> The open werre, with woundes all bibledde;

(1999–2002)

This dramatic poetry is a response not only to the warfare Chaucer himself had seen, but to disorder at all social levels, including quasi-revolutionary upheaval.

As the temple of Diana reveals, in this world of conflict and disorder even virginity is a force for violence and misery, a cause of 'vengeaunce' (2066), 'care and wo' (2072) and 'travaillynge' (2083). Although the description is deliberately cut short and obliterated in memory (2052 and 2074), this version of Diana's world is, it finally insists, depicted in 'lifly' manner (2087): this is what life is *really* like.

The process of the poem continues to contrast the dark realities of conflict and the ideological features of the aristocratic world. The massive and very expensive lists (2090) are now ready to stage the chivalric containment of disorder. The parties of Palamon and Arcite gather in stately order and splendid detail, typified by Lygurge and Emetreus, two figures deeply ferocious, as befitting tyrants, and dripping with jewels — the product and also the legitimization of their authority (2128–79). Yet all come in the cause of idealized ideology:

For trusteth wel that dukes, crlcs, kynges
Were gadered in this noble compaignye,
For love and for encrees of chivalrye.

(2182–4)

The fact that medieval magnates *did* gather in that way and *did* feel it was for those ostensible reasons only makes more real the impact of the ideology and makes its unmasking more historically potent.

The optimistic tide of the poem now ebbs back towards the dark. Each major figure visits the appropriate temple. Palamon is hopeful, and believes his prayer is granted, as a student of romance would expect. Emily, though, prays for either continued chastity or at least to go to the one who most desires her (2323–5). But this passivity is no defence from the real world and in Diana's fires she sees dreadful portents. Diana indicates that for her, as for the heroes, this 'aventure of love' will not be the ordinary romance, but will be beyond human control and be inherently destructive.

And last comes Arcite. Chaucer has altered his source's order to create a steady deterioration in mood. The Mars sequence is littered with motifs of fire, betrayal, offence, strength, battle and, again and again, fire. The final word 'Victorie', the ambiguous quest of the knight in war and love, victory over other men and over women, is set in a stark context.

That Chaucer has this negative interpretation firmly in mind is made clear by the austere, powerful and original end to Part Three. He introduces Saturn to resolve conflict between the gods, anxious about their own authorities. In a famous speech Saturn promises that he will solve things, not through Theseus-like grandeur or through the wonders of love, but by his own supervisory power over treachery, misfortune, and social chaos. The passage sums up the grim aspect of fourteenth century history and stands as the darkest moment in this realization of the reality within the imaginary world of chivalry:

Myn is the drenchyng in the see so wan;
Myn is the prison in the derke cote;
Myn is the stranglyng and hangyng by the throte,
The murmure and the cherles rebellyng,
The groynynge, and the pryvee empoysonyng;

(2456–60)

Part Four follows with a complex interweaving of the glory and the horror, the narrative realization of what has been allegorically set out in Part Three. At once royal authority is invoked through the 'feeste' (2483) and the power of love is dramatized through 'the lusty seson of that May' (2484). Then the technique of the poem closes in from such idealistic long shots to present with intimate, realistic detail the specific busy scene of preparing the tournament; yet in case it establishes its autonomous value, this human actuality is contained by the insistence that Theseus rules by public consent (2563).

The battle begins in finely arranged order; cultural order, in fact, because Chaucer calls up the method of alliterative poetry for the opening sequence; lines 2598–616 are a subtle pastiche of the thumping alliterative style that gloried in and legitimized the warrier ethos of the Germanic past. As that literary ordering fades, so does the splendour – horses fall, men tumble like balls, are hurt, captured, immobilized. The fury of the conflict is brought out and Palamon and Arcite, again like animals (2626–33), exchange 'jelous strokes' (2634), but then the superior malignancy of Saturn takes hold. Arcite is not beaten in fight, fair or unfair, but simply pitches from his horse straight on to his head, as men really do in the cursory accidents of war.

Theseus steps in to try and restore shattered chivalric order with 'alle blisse and greet solempnitee' (2702) ('solempnitee' in Middle English means splendid order not gloominess); people are confident that Arcite will survive; chivalric revel returns in a long and strained sequence of rationalization inspired by Theseus (2715–40). But all this forced optimism is destroyed by medical reality; in a passage inserted into his source, Chaucer, almost like Saturn himself, relishes the bad news from hospital:

> Swelleth the brest of Arcite and the soore
> Encreesseth at his herte moore and moore.
> The clothered blood, for any lechecraft,
> Corrupteth, and is in his bouk ylaft,
> . . .
> The pipes of his longes gonne to swelle
> And every lacerte in his brest adoun
> Is shent with venym and corrupcioun.
> Hym gayneth neither, for to gete his lif,
> Vomyt upward, ne dounward laxatif.
> All is tobrosten thilke regioun;
>
> (2743–57)

Here the techniques of close realistic detail are, as in the temple of Mars, the speech of Saturn, even the assembling of the tournament (2491–515), employed to cut the ground from beneath the ideal assurances of chivalric romance.

But the assurances are still offered. Arcite speaks with the codewords of military and amatory chivalry – 'service', 'compaignye' (twice), 'sweete foo', 'cosyn', 'servaunt' – and finally a whole series straight from the description of a knight: 'trouthe, honour, knighthode, Wysdom, humblesse, estaat and heigh kynrede, Fredom. . .' (2789–91).

But he still dies, as the narrator dismissively and abruptly says:

> His spirit chaunged hous and wente ther,
> As I cam nevere, I kan nat tellen wher.
>
> (2809–10)

The same gloomy, impotent realism is expressed by the women, who can only say, in their reduced and possession-like status:

> 'Why woldestow be deed,' thise wommen crye
> And haddest gold ynough, and Emelye?'
>
> (2835–6)

In equally inglorious but realistic form Egeus gives his banal summary, with its telling aside at the whole Canterbury frame story:

> This world nys but a thurghfare ful of wo
> And we ben pilgrymes, passynge to and fro.
>
> (2847–8)

But chivalry and royal authority are not easily dismissed. Theseus pulls himself together and launches a last assault on grim reality, with 'busy cure' to show his determination and anxiety (2853). The funeral is to be splendid at least – yet now the text weighs in against chivalric splendour, for the funeral is doubly negative. Not only is it a model of social dysfunction with the fiery destruction of a knight and the unsplendid appearance of his brother in arms (2882–4), not only are the funeral arrangements, like Mars and Saturn themselves, massively destructive of the natural world (2913–32), but the whole description is couched in the negative mode of *occupatio*: I will not describe this, says the narrator. It is a rhetorical device of epic and complex type, as commentators always say, but also one of deliberately negative impact.

In the same way and for the same purpose, Theseus's final speech is, as the recent British critics have stated, not a triumph of rational religion. He moves

> from unconvincing philosophical speculation to sensible practical advice: he has not shown that all is for the best in the world of the poem, but he has shown how to go on living in a world ruled by Saturn.[32]

All those in power can do is to recognize conflict, and try to cope with it. The dreams of romance have been penetrated by a potent poem. The text never values positively the agents of disruption, whether they are containingly presented as misfortune, or symbolized by Saturn and Mars, or generalized in the 'churles murmurynge'. But the text does reveal the existence of counter-aristocratic forces, lays bare the ideological character of the romance tradition which largely ignores them, and even admits they can have a human presence and voice. The admission is immediately followed in *The Canterbury Tales* by the sound of the churls themselves.

The Host, like Theseus, seeks to hold on to conservative order; he forgets about the draw (which he in any case manipulated), and turns to the Monk for a tale to 'quite', that is match, the Knight. But, still like Theseus, he finds competitive self-assertion crowding in as the Miller gives a distinctly hostile implication to 'quiting' the Knight. This is more than a flurry of bad manners. As Patterson has indicated, it has political implications, drawn out of the Knight's tale itself.[33] The structure of the Miller's tale makes this absolutely clear.

This story also tells how two young men compete for a woman, and how authority is overturned. Close-ups of reality brought telling disruptions in the Knight's tale, and the Miller's tale confidently stakes out a position on the terrain of vivid naturalism. This is a romance of real life, where the first lover grabs his beloved by the 'queynte' (3276), where she is a willing and sexually aware accomplice, where the competing lovers receive grotesque physical penalties, and where the genre is dirty joke, not epic romance. Fourteenth-century Oxford, not ancient Athens, is the location, in a lodging-house, not a palace. The detailed realism of the technique has made possible Bennett's detailed and distinctly reductive study of the tale in its setting —

this through its worm's eye view of historicity quite obscures the real historical function of the tale.[34]

There is more going on here than parody, that critical response which itself conceals the dynamic tension of the two tales. Nicholas, unlike Arcite, is quite happy to be 'Allone, withouten any compaignye' (3204). He likes being in private, he hatches and enacts his schemes from his lonely base and that suggests a socioeconomic context: privacy and secrecy were weapons throughout the professional group in the general prologue.

Absalon is also a figure of critical reversal. He is the more passive, lover-like figure, who sings a wonderfully grotesque version of the famous Song of Solomon love-lyric (3698–707); unlike Palamon, he is not the man who gets the girl, but the one who wields a fearful weapon of peasant's revenge. There is no profit in *fin amor* in this social world; cunning and violence bring their rewards overtly here, just as they do covertly at higher social levels.

The woman, too, is not just a parody of Emily but a deliberate establishment of peasant vitality. The famous description of Alison brings an anti-heroine into sexual life:

> Thereto she koude skippe and make game,
> As any kyde or calf folwynge his dame.
> Hir mouth was sweete as bragot or the meeth,
> Or hoord of apples leyd in hey or heeth.   (3259–62)

The sensual picture and sound of the lines is fulfilled in her knowing and active sexuality, brought to a climax in one of the great lines of feminine independence: "Tehee!" quod she and clapte the wyndow to' (3740).

The churls do mock the nobles, but not without their own values; like the 'House of Rumour' they lead a dense and noisily vital life, a productive life in all its disorder. John is a working carpenter, Alison a busy housewife, Gervays a smith with long hours, Absolon a man of all work in the parish.

The difference between the workaday productive world and aristocratic ideology is created in the form of the Miller's tale. Muscatine has explained at his persuasive best how the technique itself shapes a particular response to the world:

> It is this solidity of detail along with the characterisation intimately interlaced with it that gives the ingenious plotting its overpowering substantiality.[35]

The vigorous detail is quite different in intensity and function from the bare plot mechanics of the French fabliau — a genre used by aristocrats to ridicule the bourgeoisie. Here the details and the churls who value and handle them have their own status. The shape of the story is the subtlest part of formal meaning in the Miller's tale. As critics have shown, the Knight's tale has essentially a Gothic form, that is a two-dimensional revelation of a pre-existing meaning, and the interplay of chivalric ordering and real disorder reveals this structural principle at work.[36] The Miller's tale, though, works like the classic novel; a three-dimensional story builds up through realistic cause and effect, of a minutely detailed sort, to a physically dramatized climax. As Nicholas shouts 'Water', the carpenter makes a crucial mis-interpretation for specific reasons: time, place, plotting all cohere in material reality. The structural form insists that this is what is real — noises, actions, human motives, rather than allegory, ideals, Fortune, God — the thematic bases of the Gothic structure.

At the level of verbal style there is a similar contrast. The voice of the Knight's tale is literary and bookish, but the Miller's tale is oral, colloquial, a brilliant script to be read aloud and performed. The carpenter's garbled prayer, Alison's high excited voice, Nicholas's wheedling persuasions, the style itself states belief in a here and now of a distinctly mundane sort.

The Miller's tale then, draws attention to the reality and the inner power of the world of churls, recognized as a threat by the Knight's tale but not explored there. The conflict between the two is dynamic, and not merely because Chaucer is a fine parodist and an inspired humorist. Their relation is in classic Marxist terms dialectic; they are in historical contradiction to each other like the House of Fame and the 'House of Rumour'. It was millers and carpenters who built the splendid lists, it was university clerks who made possible the lofty speeches of Theseus and Palamon. The exploitation by the ruling classes of the productive classes gave them their ruling place, their confidence, their world; and it was the workers' exclusion from the world of chivalry that defined and made threatening their own rumbunctious world of churlish vigour and materially real culture. Finally, it is the historical weakness of that aristocratic world, its ultimate inability to enforce its rule, whether through the physical force of cavalry or the cultural force of chivalry, that makes this churlish voice one increasingly heard in the period and so a necessary, if (from a traditional viewpoint shared by the narrator) regrettable, part of a poem that imaginatively realizes historical forces.

But the realization is not itself value-free; the author does apologize, and the tale does contain its own containment. By the end of the story all the men are disabled in one way or another: Absolon is psychically ruined and Nicholas and the carpenter are unfit for their chosen spheres of action. Only Alison goes free: what in Emily was a gloomy passivity is here the power to lie back and enjoy life — or whatever comes along in it. Weissman aptly comments that Emily and Alison summarize the spectrum of Chaucer's treatment of women.[37]

Conflict without regret, animal-like fighting without the noble language of fraternity, these are by implication a discredit to the lower classes (as they were in *The Parliament of Fowls*). They will next be developed as an overt weakness. The 'churles murmurynge' grew from a reference in the Knight's tale into a poetic riot in the Miller's response; now dissension among the 'churles' is developed into a savage and debilitating conflict, through the medium of the Miller's colleague on the ideal manor, his bitter enemy in disorderly reality, the Reeve.

The Miller's tale is received with delight, but the Reeve feels he must defend his own trade of carpentry by belittling that of millers. Craft solidarity, that threatening aspect of the productive classes, is realized only to be neutralized by conflict between trades, the opposite of class consciousness. Another threatening formation, more overt in the period, is raised and resolved in the rich headlink to the Reeve's tale. The notion that he resembled priest or friar (general prologue 590 and 621) is here pursued in his meditation on age (3867–87). A man of shrewdness rather than brawn, his lower class threat moves towards Lollardy, a force that in the period was frequently seen to be related to peasant uprising.[38] The Host jumps in religious terms on the possibility – 'The devel made a reve for to preche' (3903), and the Reeve withdraws to a simply physical anger, stating plainly the text's slightly ominous sense of conflict between views and people: 'For leveful is with force force of-showve' (3912).

His tale is forceful indeed. It shows how a miller's intended dupes actually humiliate him through his wife and only daughter

— as with Theseus and John the carpenter, property and patriarchy are vulnerable together. Like its predecessor, the tale has meaning far beyond its teller's personality. It establishes at once a pattern of disorderly, role-abandoning social attitudes. The miller is both a good businessman and a thief, seeking his own profit and his family's social ascent. In this he has an ally: his wife is the daughter of the local parson who feels that 'holy chirches good' (3983) should follow his definitely illegal family. This nasty collocation of sinful parson, snobbish wife and grasping tradesman lacks the sprightly vigour of the Miller's tale. The Reeve's tale in its venom, its somewhat spare realization of lower-class life, its biting picture of hostility and malice is much closer to the traditional aristocratic anti-bourgeois fabliau than the preceding tale. And this convergence of church and churl, while morally reprehensible, is politically much less threatening than priests and peasants in combination, whether merely Lollard or actually revolutionary.

In the Reeve's tale the productive classes are seen without vitality or value. The plot itself is without potent imagination and the characters are merely two-dimensional. The device by which the miller first fools the clerks is puerile — he just lets go their horse; but equally their own triumph is one of opportunism and luck in a darkened bedroom, with no trace of Nicholas's fantastic scheming, Absolon's ambition or indeed of Alison's vital sense of fun.

The clerks have some individuation in speaking in dialect — the first example in English literature — and they bear what values exist in this tale. Much more firmly tied to their university than Nicholas ever was, not involved as he was in lower class life, they merely conquer the churls and withdraw to their privileged place. The tale operates in a much more conservative way than its pedecessor, both by its internal character and by its presence as evidence of debilitating disruption within the forces of social disorder.

A further stage in lower class self-destruction appears to be the idea behind the Cook's tale. This unappealing servant of the bourgeoisie delights in the Reeve's vision of brutal chaos and arouses the Host to instigate a conflict that was no doubt long-standing between his own trade and the Cook's — more craft contention. The Cook's 'quiting' of the Reeve, is clearly going to operate at a newly debased level. His story of a depraved London apprentice breaks off with startlingly direct words about the wife of the hero's friend who 'swyved for hir sustenance' (4422). This is a new climax of churlish disgustingness in this verbal peasant revolution against decency and linguistic order.

That shocking statement is the end of what is called Group A (or Fragment I). Chaucer's next plans remain obscure, whether to complete this tale or have it interrupted, as happens twice later on (to the Monk and to Chaucer himself). One category of manuscripts, with a very early origin, uses as a second Cook's tale 'The Tale of Gamelyn', a stirring romance about a disinherited youngest son who joins up with outlaws and wins his rights through distinctly rough justice. Some have thought Chaucer had the poem among his papers intending to work it up for a pilgrim: it might have suited the Yeoman, and so provide an apt conservative portrayal of a faithful retainer projecting the image of churlish violence on behalf of the landowning class.

That can be no more than conjecture. But a containment of a kind is applied to this opening section of class disorder, namely the Man of Law's tale. It appears to be a directly conservative re-enactment of authority by those in power, a lawyer's response to the lawyer-baiting disorder of the Peasants' Revolt. The connections of the Man of Law's tale have consistently been sought in the subsequent material, because of its puzzling endlink, of which there is no satisfactory version. But the tale also follows Group A, and a socially attuned understanding of the tales, which recognizes the political conflict being realized in the group, can see just why the Man of Law's tale is an appropriate continuation, a strong foreclosure of the disturbing implications of the noisy churlish murmuring. Such a view can also see how the Wife of Bath opens up such a challenge again, and that authority and disruption alternate throughout the great sequence from her prologue through to the Pardoner's tale.[39]

The Host calls on the lawyer as a man of some status — he is selected after the Knight and, abortively, the Monk. He comes from the professional group, and typically of such people he has cultural interests — including, in a sharply self-conscious moment, Chaucer's own work (47–76). But that group was led by the Merchant and the lawyer has, at base, strongly mercantile attitudes and connections. When he discusses that 'hateful harm, condicion of poverte' (99), his own position is hate-filled. He judges that poverty leads people to abuse Christ for the way in which he 'misdeparteth richesse temporal' (107): wise people feel that death is better than this perverting poverty (114) and so everybody should avoid the state (119) as do those 'noble' and 'prudent folk', the 'riche marchauntz' (122–3). The lawyer's own literary and cultural authority, an ideology slides aside to reveal his true nature, as the 'seeming' motif of the general prologue suggested. The lawyer says, apparently without self-doubt, that he would have no tales at all had not a merchant told him this one — and it is a story itself initiated by merchants, who make the grotesque marriage between the daughter of the Christian emperor and the brutish Moslem.

The inherent conservatism of the story of Constance has been noted by Delany:

> To Chaucer's courtly patrons, employers and friends, the tale of Constance . . . must have been a welcome reaffirmation of the hierarchical values which had been so recently and sharply attacked.[40]

That is certainly the drift of the tale, but those in the audience who paid close attention to the introduction would not perhaps relish the position from which it was launched, essentially one of crass mercantilism. A more securely founded conservatism will emerge later in the tales, from Melibee onwards.

Part of the ideological impact of the Man of Law's tale is that a queen is the figure of patience, constancy and, finally, of triumph. This familiar romance narrative re-asserts thematically the primacy of the upper reaches of society: its topic is firmly conservative. The story also opposes in its highly formal mode the tales of the churls — the technical fabric of high culture is itself being rebuilt along with its ideology. Like the Knight's tale this story is set back in time, not in a real and English present. Its mode of presentation is distinctly two-dimensional and without detailed realism or human close-ups, relying on sudden and sensational developments like the death of the nameless 'false knight' for falsely swearing that Constance is guilty. The divine hand that 'hym smoot uppon the nekke-boon' (669) is an archetype of Gothic art, far from the human cause and effect of the churlish narratives. Delany sums up the mode by saying Constance operates 'as an agglomeration of virtues rather than as a recognisable person.[41]

So one structure of meaning in the tale is to impose aristocratic conservatism and a lofty model of patience on a decreasingly visible poor, and this acts strongly in containment of the tales' predecessors. But once at least this tale has a decided moment of strain, revealing the ideological character of its impact. The only often-quoted passage is the vivid simile of Constance looking like a man bound for execution:

> Have ye nat seyn somtyme a pale face,
> Among a prees, of hym that hath be lad
> Toward his deeth, wher as hym gat no grace,
> And swich a colour in his face hath had
> Men myghte knowe his face that was bistad,
> Amonges all the faces in that route?

(645–50)

The moment is one of pathos for Constance, but its depth comes from close human observation and sympathy, feeling for the victim of oppression — features that have been almost completely written out of the Man of Law's tale in order to obscure the very politics with which those responses are enmeshed.

Another type of politics is inherent in the Man of Law's tale, one that feminist criticism has brought to notice in recent years. The story is about a woman who is suffering as a woman and as a mother in particular. The genre of the story is 'The accused queen', and Schlauch sees criticism of tyranny in the brutality of kings throughout the story.[12] That is undoubtedly so, but the impact is upon a woman, not upon a state or a class. Constance's power and qualities are not in themselves disorderly, for she is an aristocrat, and saints' legends and moral works consistently allow a strong role for women as exemplars of virtue. But in using such a structure to contain the preceding social disorder, the tale has also raised the possibility of female power. That explodes out of Constance's conservative context into a real, demotic and above all experiential world as Wife of Bath begins to speak. The material and themes of the opening sequence of the poem, based as it is on social conflict, are themselves developed powerfully in the second sequence, which projects the historical imagination through human types to a rare level of power and complexity.

III From the Wife of Bath's prologue to the Pardoner's tale: 'Experience, though noon auctoritee Were in this world . . .'

Reduced by humanist criticism to an entertaining and slightly alarming literary character, the Wife of Bath is a remarkable medium of many aspects of sociohistorical insight. A woman of independent mind and body who is also a successful small manufacturer is a striking combination of threats to conservative male stasis. She is a fully credible contemporary figure, a profit-making producer from one of the new industrial regions.[43] The cultural attitudes represented through her are equally potent and innovative: she stands consciously for the value of experience over authority (1–3) — the terms refer primarily to systems of knowledge and proof, but they inevitably spread (as *The Book of Fame* indicates) to mean the validity of ordinary people's opinions and lives against those in authority. That matter will be developed later in the tale; for the moment the authority in question is that of the church.

The opening sequence of the Wife's prologue, up to the Pardoner's interruption (163), turns clerical authority upside down to argue the feminist cause through a knowledge of the traditional materials of anti-feminist diatribe. The mode of approach is itself contemporary: Robertson, one of those best qualified to know, calls it a 'mock-Lollard sermon'.[44] The Lollards were against the physical wealth and power of the church and for the individual Christian. That too is a matter that will surface in the tale; here the point is that as a woman making a stand against an oppressive church with learning and vigour, her approach is convergent with a major force of innovation, one that was not in the period readily distinguished from civil dissent.[45]

The usual literary critical approach to the wife merely validates its own bourgeois individualism, seeing her as a bold free spirit, and ignoring her historical and social context. Nor does it see the difficult and slow development throughout her prologue of what modern consciousness so readily and gratefully identifies as a subjective voice.

The opening sequence, after all, does no more than establish a position by reversing a clerical approach. Through this are developed elements of a statement about the self — the Wife uses the first person a good deal; from her initial negative positioning a sense of a private will and role is constructed as well as a specifically feminine experience:

> He spak to hem that wolde lyve parfitly;
> And lordynges, by youre leve, that am nat I
> I wol bistowe the flour of al myn age
> In the actes and in fruyt of mariage.
>
> (111–14)

After the Pardoner's ineffective interruption, the prologue continues in a way which is more experience-oriented, but by no means autobiographical in terms of novelistic realism. The famous account of life with old husbands is in fact a quasi-allegorical speech which develops out of a general statement of life with the type 'old husband'. But the pressure of real experience bears down on the still idealized mode. Even though she is quoting a typical speech to an archetypal old man, the Wife is dealing with human experience; it has not yet found its self-expressive mode or genre, but is asserting its force with remarkable vigour:

> Thou seist that oxen, asses, hors, and houndes,
> They been assayed at diverse stoundes;
> Bacyns, lavours, er that men hem bye,
> Spoones and stooles, and al swich housbondrye
> And so been pottes, clothes and array;
>
> (285–9)

It may sound as if these objects are flying across the kitchen, but the actualization of a woman's experience is not yet fully formed.

It becomes more so when she talks of one particular husband, her fourth; though the opening sequence is distinctly traditional, it does bring self-consciousness and direct experience to the forefront of the poem and makes domestic metaphor the basis of the famous passage:

> Unto this day it dooth my herte boote
> That I have had my world as in my tyme.
> But age, allas! that al wole envenyme,
> Hath me biraft my beautee and my pith.
> Lat go, farewel! the devel go therwith!
> The flour is goon, ther is namoore to telle;
> The bren, as I best kan, now moste I selle.
>
> (472–8)

A courageous, self-conscious, domestic and mercantile person has emerged — it has been a powerful dramatic creation, wriggling out of the restrictive genre of literary authority as it does out of patriarchy and clerical oppression.

The final sequence of the prologue, the memoir of life with Jankyn, is in the fully formed new style of individual voice and feminine consciousness. The Wife relates her experience, so explaining her knowledge of the anti-feminist clerics — motivation, as in the Miller's tale, is basic to this new experiential mode. The climax is developed fully through action and reaction, the very stuff of humanist fiction:

> And whan I saugh he wolde nevere fyne
> To reden on this cursed book al nyght,
> Al sodeynly thre leves have I plyght
> Out of his book, right as he radde, and eke
> I with my fest so took hym on the cheke
> That in oure fyr he fil bakward adoun.
> And he up stirte as dooth a wood leoun,
> And with his fest he smoot me on the heed,
> That in the floor I lay as I were deed.

> (788–96)

Jankyn gives her freedom and command (819–21), but she immediately says that she was 'to hym as kynde As any wyf from Denmark unto Ynde.' (823–4). Does this mean that having been given authority, she did not exercise it – an ideological rejection by text and author of a hard-won position? If so, it is brief, and has hardly affected the vigorous personality and practices of the figure of female power. Rather, her actions suggest that woman creates a better order than masculine hegemony, for now she was 'also trewe, and so was he to me' (825).

The admission that she is sovereign is, of course, the dramatic climax, and in the historical context would be the sticking point. Robertson and Haskell have shown that medieval women did in fact have considerable power and authority when they worked within the official system of male authority.[46] But as Haskell shows starkly, when women actually insisted on authority, trouble followed. Three of the Paston women stood out for marriage of their own choice. One was beaten by her parents, imprisoned, and languished until a new marriage was found; one married her lover and was ostracized for life; one eventually gave in to her parents' wishes. Entertaining and lively as the Wife is, her figure has in its grasp social revolution within the family — just as in its economic position it is a product of a new socioeconomic world.

The Friar, that exploiter of women physically and financially, objects that a 'dame' should preach (831). Like a reeve rising against a miller, his own kind conflicts with him when Summoner speaks hotly against friars, but that bout is deferred. First the Wife disposes of friars as mobile, sexually impotent pests — the tone of the poetry has the domestic density of the old-husband abuse (864–81). To her new vigour is attached an old tale of King Arthur's world. Some commentators have thought Chaucer implies that the Wife is provincial in taste, linking this with sarcasm about romance in the Nun's Priest's tale (p. 143). The negative element, though, is not so much a comment on a provincial woman (a modern, metropolitan reading) but lies in the understanding of the repressive essence of romance.

Three basic elements in this romance are projected as threats rather than, as is more usual, accepted as natural: the violence of the hero, the power of a woman to mediate the resolution of his distress, the isolation and individualism of the hero. Each of these is amplified to a point of crisis, where the normal romance offers them as basic situations with some threatening features, which are all resolved by the mechanism of the plot and the overriding ideology of chivalry, martial and amatory.[47]

Here the violence is done to a woman: a knight rapes a girl. Feminine power is not the banal mediation of love-service leading to a hand-over of property: it is, rather, judicial authority and real wisdom. Told as it is from a feminine viewpoint, the gradients of romance are steepened and the hero stripped of all power but to offend, learn, complain, be berated and yield.

Chaucer's historical imagination revives the ancient structure of the 'sovereignty' story, in which the woman represents the sovereignty of the tribe or nation which the new king marries and so possesses. That Celtic matrilinear (but not matriarchal) pattern is dissipated in Christian society, and the fairy mistress becomes no more than a force of masculine wish-fulfilment in romances like *Sir Launfal* — or indeed Chaucer's own 'Sir Thopas'. But in a text where women could be recognized as having real authority, as practitioners of a craft and as wealthy widows, true sovereignty surfaces again. The story is not only conscious of female power, but of the historical changes that make that power newly possible and radically effective.

This social pattern develops slowly in the story. The authority of the queen to judge a rapist and of the wise old woman to know what women want is, after all, no more than a type of sexual apartheid. If that is all women's power adds up to, then there are many, indeed most, areas where men will still rule. But when the old wife addresses her husband on what he has done wrong, the poem moves to a different plane, seeing women as a force for liberation from a whole world of masculine and aristocratic oppression, suggesting a new world of social and ethical values. The narrative gives this viewpoint a special weight because it provides the resolution to the knight's deepened distress.

The story becomes socialized from the point at which feminine power really does affect his life and his understanding of his life. In return for her wisdom he must marry the old woman. This brings shame to him and alienates him from the social world natural to a knight and man of honour, even from humanity as he conceives it:

> For prively he wedded hire on the morwe,
> And al day after hidde him as a owle,
> So wo was hym, his wyf looked so foule.

> (1080–2)

But his enforced privacy, this negative of traditional social values, is inverted by the wise wife into a new positive as she lectures him on true 'gentillesse':

> Looke who that is moost vertuous alway,
> Pryvee and apert, and moost entendeth ay
> To do the gentil dedes that he kan;
> Taak hym for the grettest gentil man.

> (1113–16)

This is a truer system of evaluation that that which is linked to 'old richesse' (1110 and 1118), it is not inherited like manorial 'honour' — a name for both the ideal concept and property itself. This value has its own cultural reinforcement and authorities to back its experiential value: first that of Christ (1117–18), then Dante (1125–30). The point is not a passing one; it is emphasized, supported, and restated with lucid power:

For, God it woot, men may wel often fynde
A lordes sone do shame and vileynye;
. . .
For vileyns sinful dedes make a cherl.
. . .
Thy gentillesse cometh fro God allone.
Thanne comth oure verray gentillese of grace;
It was no thyng biquethe us with oure place.

(1150–64)

Experience is now not just a stick to beat male clerics with, or a vivid new genre of narrative. It is a religiously-based evaluative system and mode of behaviour. Brewer has commented on the potentially revolutionary character of the topics raised in this speech[48] and it looks forward to the foundation of bourgeois morality, that rationalization of individual behaviour and mystification of the less appealing aspects of mercantile relations. Weber and Tawney both wrote at length on the connection; Chaucer has developed it out of this dissenting female industrialist quasi-Lollard, a striking sign of how far his historical imagination can reach.

This repositioning of the whole debate between churls and 'gentils' does not pass, however, without its own containment. The old woman moves on to poverty and gives a conservative and quietist treatment that is much more potent than the brutal dismissal by the Man of Law, and which is also in line with Langland's conservative presentation of 'Patient Poverty'. The old wife talks of 'glad poverte' and with subtle manipulation asserts that

Poverte is this, although it seme alenge,
Possessioun that no wight wol chalenge.

(1199–200)

The comment re-establishes possession as a value, though she actually dispossessed it in her previous speech. That sequence spoke about real deeds, but this passage reverts to an allegorical treatment: 'Verray poverte, it syngeth proprely' (1191). The equally conservative but very brief discussion of old age, relies solely on old world systems of knowledge and value — it appeals to common knowledge among 'ye gentils of honour' (1209) and asserts that plenty of 'auctoritee' is available (1212).

So the old woman's speech rapidly withdraws from its

revolutionary potential, both in theme and in mode. As it pulls back within conservative cultural practices, so in the action she is regressive. Given the choice, he yields it to her, but she rejects sovereignty more plainly than the Wife did at the end of the prologue; not only will she be beautiful all the time and faithful all the time, she is his property entirely: 'Dooth with my lyf and deth right as yow lest' (1248).

That extreme containment of her established position as woman and as social commentator is itself not achieved without residual strain. The choice that she sets the knight is not the traditional one. That was always couched in terms of an honour/shame culture; he had to choose her beautiful either at night or in the day — private pleasure or public honour, never both. Chaucer sets up a choice which remains on the terrain she established: he must choose her beautiful and fickle, or ugly and unfaithful — that is, he must suffer privately from either her ugliness or his knowledge of her infidelity.

In the same subliminally threatening way, as the Wife ends her complex story a radical voice is heard again:

> . . . and Jhesu Crist us sende
> Housbondes meeke, yonge, and fressh abedde,
> And grace t'overbyde hem that we wedde;
> And eek I praye Jhesu shorte hir lyves
> That wol nat be governed by hir wyves;
> And olde and angry nygardes of dispence,
> God sende hem soone verray pestilence!

(1258–64)

The voice is aware of sexual power and vitality — outliving, overbearing those who wield notional authority. It also claims to speak straight to Christ and demands to handle money for itself. After the complex development of the female position into a new social possibility, after the brusque and somewhat unconvincing containment of the end, the poem finally insists that the voice is still audible, conflict goes on in society and in history.

After the Wife ends, the Friar briefly amplifies his dismissal of her as a preacher and then hurries on to his real enemy, his rival in exploitation, the Summoner. Their economic struggle is explored in the tale, which goes far beyond personal feeling into a telling socioeconomic projection of the acquisitive ideas of both

Summoner and Friar. The story of a vicious summoner is based on a fable of the 'devil tricks the villain' type. But the world of fourteenth century experience comes through in telling and painful detail;[49] the mode is that of the Miller's and Reeve's tales, but the impact of brawling, greedy, money-obsessed people within the church is like the harsher world of the Reeve.

Through the structure and language of the tale it becomes clear that the summoner's true error is not just that he misuses his power for his own ends, and especially not just that he seeks sexual favours, but that he uses his knowledge of sexual life to gain money. He is a cash- and exchange-involved person, not continuing the long tradition of a manorial or use economy, within which the church operated as a landholder with its own traditional rights to a tenth (or tithe) of production. The summoner does not fulfil his role in the chain of quasi-manorial duty:

> His master hadde but half of his duetee

> (1352)

Here 'duetee' is understood as money, and so can be appropriated. He himself had no rent, but bribes (1373).

Although vocabulary and action together define him as an extra-feudal force, he pretends to be within that world when he mets the diabolic 'yeman'; he claims to be a 'bailly' or steward, who is going 'to reysen up a rente That longeth to my lordes duetee' (1390-1), feudal terms the text has firmly denied to him. The words that the summoner uses and are used by the devil as he entraps him are firmly within the cash-nexus; the summoner is a creature of that world of exchange values that Marx discusses in 'The Chapter on Money' in the *Grundrisse*.[50] Contemporary usage shows that 'extorcioun' (1439) refers especially to money-based pressure, that 'dispence' (1432) is consistently expenditure of cash and that 'purchas' (1451) in particular means both seizure and profit, personal gain; the language points to a whole series of self-seeking and non-manorial practices.

The devil, though he can speak the language of exchange values, works firmly within the manorial world of use value. Like any feudal figure, he relies on valid oaths — not the carter's, but those of the summoner and the old woman. He is true 'bailly' for God, despite himself, and the summoner is finally won not as profit but as the devil's man — in a feudal relationship. The devil's own language helps to create this pattern: when he says in rejecting the cart that he wins nothing 'upon cariage' (1570), he is not only making a neat joke, he is referring to the manorial right of cartage.

In the general prologue the Summoner said, in self-justification, 'Purs is the ercedekenes helle' (658), and that connection is made by this other summoner. He, the Friar says:

> . . . koude somne, on peyne of Cristes curs,
> And they were glade for to fille his purs,

> (1347–8)

The rhyme 'curs/purs' comes grimly true, and the man who uses his ability as a summoner to break oaths and duties and merely gain cash profit is caught in a web of fidelity by a morè powerful true steward. The tale acts out a deep and structural irony about the disruptive impact of people like the summoner in the church and in traditional economic society.

The Summoner opens return fire with no pretence of anything but rage and hatred for the Friar. But that personal motivation is merely an initiating moment; the story that is told, like the Friar's, has a considerable degree of autonomy from its violent teller. It undergoes a slow, subtle development and details the mechanics of corruption through the actions of the friar it describes. This tale is the practical and specific complement to its predecessor's general theory of commodity-oriented man.

The story opens with an account of how friars preach against regular clergy in order to earn rewards in kind – 'mele and chese, or elles corn' (1739). But this use-value world is not the friars' true terrain — they wipe out the names of their beneficiaries as they move on; the telling nature of the comment is underlined when the listening Friar objects only to that point (1761).

As the friar continues to act in the story, negative evaluation closes around him. He is presented in increasingly fabliau-like physical and so non-ideal detail — he flicks the cat off the bench familiarly as he settles down to talk and beg (1775). The realism grows more and more like the hypocritical acquisitiveness of the Friar in the general prologue. This friar kisses the wife as more than a confesser (1804), he attacks the regular clergy too radically for belief and over-reaches his own heroics in a line that places himself right in the New Testament: 'I walke, and fisshe Cristen mennes soules' (1820). Increasing attention is being paid to food by both friar and poem (e.g. 1839) and the 'Freynsshe' language flows out (1832, 1838), fulfilling in dramatic form the general prologue pattern. This friar, like the summoner of the previous tale, offers himself as a quasi-manorial steward, seeking Christ's 'propre rente' (1821), but the love of coin grows on him and he cannot resist being drawn when Thomas talks about the cash cost of all this holy begging. He surges into a highly emotive harangue, a litany of coinage:

> A! yif that covent half a quarter otes!
> A! yif that covent foure and twenty grotes!
> A! yif that frere a peny, and lat hym go!

> (1963–5)

After a long, self-validating burst of correct preaching, the friar demands the chance to confess Thomas as if to offer him a professional service for his coin. Thomas refuses, so the friar asks straight out for the 'gold' (2099). All the skill of what Thomas thinks of as 'false dissymulacioun' (2123) cannot hide the naked greed, and once more a final humiliation is invoked by the obsession with coin. Thomas manages to suggest that he has his purse in his trousers, 'in pryvetee' (2143) — a dangerous word in a medieval socioeconomic context.

All that happens, of course, is that the friar receives no more than a smelly homonym of the 'ferthyng' he previously rejected (1967) and that, according to the general prologue, he would always have, 'er he wente' (255). Like Absolon he is outraged by a shame-making fart and so he complains to the lord of the village, the manorial authority, to defend the 'hooly covent' against this churlish insult (2182–3).

The ending activates this old world social force against the friar; the lord himself enjoys the joke in 'ars-metrike' (2222) and relishes his 'nyce, proude cherl' (2227), who has made an active judgement on the love of filthy lucre. The lord's squire projects the joke further with a mock-legal division of the fart through the distinctly non-financial device of a cartwheel — the world of collective feudal relations and rural objects closes in around the cash-based friar who has developed into an ogre of the exchange economy.

The stories told by Summoner and Friar are not a mere personal exchange, as critics have usually thought; the characters are used as a starting point for a powerful analysis of socioeconomic reality and change, an imaginative projection of the concrete historical roles this sort of figure was fulfilling.

The Host calls on the Clerk for a tale, the immediate role of which is to restore clerical dignity and the authority of an orthodox learned voice after the Friar degraded the status of a 'maistre'. The tale also turns out to be about marriage, and the influential critic Kittredge called the sequence from Wife to Franklin a 'marriage group'.[51] The main objection to this view is not the lack of connection in the group. In spite of the gaps between Summoner and Clerk and again between Merchant and Squire, there is no substantial break of sense, and very little finishing work was needed: the best manuscripts indicate that the order, if not authorial, can at least be regarded as authoritative.[52]

If this can readily be accepted as a technical 'group', the idea that its topic is marriage must be much more doubtful. It has already been argued that the Wife's tale makes marriage both an issue and a medium of broader social forces; that argument will be continued about all the rest of the tales in the group. The fact of the churlish brawl between Friar and Summoner makes it clear that Chaucer is not isolating a theme from its social and economic matrix, as Kittredge implied. In the sequence from Wife to Franklin marriage is a recurring topic, but so was love, or lust, in the opening sequence of the tales, and so will be families of a different sort in the long group from Shipman to Nun's Priest. If there is any identifying quality in the so-called 'marriage group', it lies in the depth and complexity of its realization of contemporary forces, and this runs on into the following tales of the Physician and Pardoner. This powerful series broadens immensely the thrust of the opening sequence; it appears to create a text of such sociohistorical veracity that the narrowing and containing impact of the following group is invoked by it.

This large and extremely potent set of tales realizes threats and counter-threats, types of social reality and their interactions, and the Wife's dynamic feminine and individual force is the dramatic opening statement. To this the Clerk's tale replies with similar power, but with a great difference in style, genre and ideological impact.

The Clerk's tale is a strange one, that gives modern readers difficulty, but once the *Tales* are seen in sociohistorical terms it takes its evident place as a paean to authority and obedience − of women and peasants especially. So it re-emphasizes the conservative position that the Man of Law's tale realized, in response to the social and familial challenges raised through the figure of the Wife of Bath. Also like the lawyer's tale, the scholar's story is old, weighty with classical, not medieval, learning — and it too seems in some ways inadequate as a response to disorder.

Walter, Marquis of Saluces, is rich and powerful, and has thorough control over his regime: 'obeisant . . . Were alle his liges' (66–7). His power is variously legitimized, by providence and people alike:

> Biloved and drad, thurgh favour of Fortune,
> Bothe of his lordes and of his commune.
>
> (69–70)

Yet as a feudal lord, he is incomplete; he has no wife, no succession. He is no more than an individual, and that is inconsistent with his position. His people feel this most, gripped as they are by dread and love, and urge him to reproduce himself and so his authority.

But there is something disturbing about the people's desire to guide the lord's reproduction; the doubt about the people's representative points to the problem and also locates it in the ambivalent parliamentary context of the late fourteenth century — they choose one 'that wisest was of loore — Or elles that the lord best wolde assente' (87–8). Walter, as autocrat, will have none of this; he says he will accede to their wish but will make the choice himself, and binds the people in rigorous obedience both to the future wife and, in particular, to himself (164–75). Aspects of tyranny are being raised and examined here, as Aers points out.[53] The chosen marriage symbolizes the total power of the lord over his distinctly manorial world, and his own appropriation of its best and most productive features. When he selects the most beautiful, faithful and hard-working (225–7) of girls from among her 'felawes' (281–2), an unexceptionable *droit de seigneur* is enacted.

Things go well for the newly socialized lord; he sees that virtue does hide under low degree, and that Griselda is not only an obedient wife but a valuable creator of 'commune profit' (431). But he cannot believe in her 'sadnesse', her ability to persevere in humble obedience — that quality so patently lacking in Griselda's peasant analogues in the late fourteenth century. So the tests begin, and they too, like marriage, are images of appropriation and authority. When Griselda is separated from her own conscious productivity in her children, like any faithful peasant, she endures the lord's will, though with sorrow:

> But natheless so sad stidefast was she
> That she endured al adversitee,

(564–5)

and she is 'evere in oon ylike sad and kynde' (602). The sentimental modern meanings of 'sad' and 'kind' have overlaid the firmly social meaning of these words and of the action so far.

Griselda, through her peasant endurance and obedience, behaves as if everything is natural — and so lordly authority is naturalized. Life proceeds, a son is born, thanks are given. But this is not the impact of the story: the tension between lord and underlings is the fault line on which this tale perilously stands, and Walter again puts on the pressure of cruel appropriation, of the son this time. As he does so the story begins to retract and explain away its severity, here in likening his actions to any malicious husband (622–3). There will be many of these mollifications of the stark structure before the Clerk stops speaking.

Appropriation of productivity is followed, in the pattern of exploitation, by abandonment when unproductive, and this is Griselda's third trial. She is to be replaced by a younger and more suitable wife. Tremors of experiential existence at the peasant level are recognized — she had 'wyl' and 'libertee' before she married him (656) and her father opposed the marriage anyway (904). To him she returns, still a model of sufferance — and also a model of womanly suffering (934–8), in another rationalizing and defusing aside, where the strain is evident as the Clerk himself corrects clerks on this matter.

Finally Griselda is seen as 'mooste servysable of alle' when she comes to help her supplanter, 'to serve and plese in my degree' (979 and 969). As the story reaches this patently unnatural climax, its tone begins to strain against itself: the extremity of the political model being offered is steadily withdrawn but not before it reaches its polemical height in the attack on the 'peple' for hailing the new Marchioness and so 'commendynge the markys governaunce':

O stormy peple! unsad and ever untrewe!
Ay undiscreet and chaungynge as a fane!
Delitynge ever in rumbul that is newe,
For lyk the moone ay wexe ye and wane.
Ay ful of clappyng, deere ynogh a jane!
Youre doom is fals, youre constance yvele preeveth;
A ful greet fool is he that on yow leeveth.

(995–1001)

It is a strangely paradoxical statement. The people are seen as fickle, like moon, coin and weathervane — and by implication like the insurgents of 1381. But their error is that they follow the whims of the autocrat. Strangely ironic reversals seem to be happening within this conservative fable; it appears to be running out of the steam of self-confidence and soon will despair altogether of its own values. Motifs of doubt and inauthenticity gather. No aristocrat could bear the strain Griselda has carried, she says (1042). She did not even wonder at the testing (1058); Walter's son will never test his wife in this way (1138). The starkly conservative material of the story is receding into a fabulous and so euphemizing distance. As the conclusion begins, it is said that no modern woman could stand such a test (1142–4); to justify the story it must now be allegorized, and that at two levels. The first is political: the tale is told

. . . that every wight, in his degree,
Sholde be constant in adversitee

(1145–6)

And that moral generalization, to obscure social oppression, permits the further idealization into Christian allegory — we should behave to God as Griselda did to Walter (1149–62). The strain of that rationalization is startling, whether or not a reader knows that in the history of the tale Walter is usually a devil.

If 'governaunce' and 'vertuous suffraunce' can finally be applied to no more than God's authority (1161–2) then the weight of the story has been relieved, especially as a response to the social and marital pressure on conventional order presented through the Wife of Bath. In the original conclusion it seems that Chaucer left it there, with that distinctly slender and tendentious Christian resolution of a socially aligned tale (the pattern to be found again in Melibee, p. 139). The 'Host stanza' (printed by

Robinson as 1212 a–g) rapidly concluded the tale after 1162, but a later, expanded ending testifies to the strain the conservative tale creates against the other tales and in the period. First, it says Griseldas are rare enough now, and puts that in a metaphor of coinage redolent of the new world of cash-nexus and non-feudal relations (1166–9). Then the whole thing is brought back to the symbolic power of the Wife, in poetry which is suddenly vigorous, ironical and image-filled. The flat, conservative banality of the Clerk's tale is overturned in a riot of marital conflict:

> Ye archewyves, stondeth at defense,
> Syn ye be strong as is a greet camaille;
> Ne suffreth nat that men yow doon offense
> And sklendre wyves, fieble as in bataille,
> Beth egre as is a tygre yond in Ynde;
> Ay clappeth as a mille, I yow consaille.

(1195–200)

The clerk finally carnivalizes his tale, in just the way that Bakhtin argues that Rabelais subverts later medieval stasis and conservatism through cultural means.[54] The impossibility of cool, scholarly, manorial theory and practice has been exposed; like Theseus's attempt at order, the scholar's contribution is both the product of an exhausted world and itself exhausted, supplanted by new vigour which is decidely not in the whimsical control of a hereditary Marquis. Imposing as it does a silence on both lower class freedom and the realistic mode, the tale's conservative censorship is finally ruptured and the conflicting voice of the experiential world bursts in. It is that voice that is picked up, in the Clerk's last words, by a very unideal figure, the Merchant.

From the Merchant's position, the Clerk's subversive 'envoy' is no more or less than reality, like the Host's view in the original, cancelled ending of the Clerk's tale (1212 a–g). The Merchant, this very rich but somewhat superficial figure of the new world, has just married; his private life is out of control, just as are, from a traditional viewpoint, his professional practices. Rich and vulgar, powerful and abhorrent, that pattern is realized in both theme and form of his tale. The tale is a full response to the Clerk's: it too is about a decision to marry and its results, but where the Clerk represented the values of the past world in ultimately unacceptable but coherent action, the Merchant's tale is a representation of the chaotic impact of a new world where the cultural values of the old world are treated as nothing more than superstructual elements, with the coarse, disorderly and exploitative reality of the new socioeconomic structure showing painfully through in this most tonally strained of all the tales.

The Merchant's tale presents the world of knightly marriage so corrupted by mercantile practices that it has neither manorial values or even low-class vitality; its plot is a fabliau that degrades all parties — an old, grotesque and finally complaisant husband, a conniving, betraying wife who goes to any extreme for sexual relief, a faithless squire who acts like his master's dog (2014) but is no more than a 'lechour, in the tree' (2257). The love letter ripped and floating in a cesspit (1954) is a symbol of what people do to each other in a world in which, as Marx outlined, commodities being the fetishized bearers of value, people treat each other like commodities.[55]

If that were all there is in the Merchant's tale, it would be like an upmarket version of the Reeve's tale. But Chaucer has, with the power of the major artist, projected the social and economic drama at the level of literary style. It is not just that January claims to be a knight and husband, that May and Damian ape lady and squire. The poem itself presents the authentic language and imagery of those roles, rich in European tradition — and like the love letter, tears them and pitches them in the excremental world of commodity relations.

When January thinks about a wife he is, of course, much too old for normal aristocratic practice. In any case, he does not think about a wife in the 'correct' way, as a producer of children, an augmenter and transmitter of the family, its 'name' and honour. He sees a wife as profit on capital:

> Thanne is a wyf the fruyt of his tresor
>
> (1270)

He speaks at some length about the benefits of marriage, and his actual position is slowly revealed as the speech progresses. January is increasingly concerned about the threat a wife poses to him, a moneyed individual — his mercantile stance creates the problem in this new venture. He disapprovingly quotes Theophrastes on a wife's acquisitive and oppressive force (1296–1306), but as the speech unfolds that is clearly his own fear. A wife will outlast the husband (1317–18); she will keep his goods (1343);

she will rule (1357 and 1361); a humble wife is best (or, the other side of the words, nothing will best even a humble wife, 1375); she will command and you will suffer (1378); she will keep your husbandry — that is, will tend it in your life and have it after your death (1380); finally, harm is especially unlikely to come to wives (1392).

January, the possessive individual, nevertheless imitates a familial aristocrat, and calls together his council. His position is clear. He wants something young and toothsome, good meat not old straw (1419–22); he wants a pliable thing like wax, and though he does recognize reproductive power, this is only valuable so that his 'heritage', which here means no more than money, does not go to a stranger (1438–40). Councils are meant to advise the powerful, not be a rubber stamp (Melibee will assemble a positive model). Here January has the worst aspect of an aristocratic council; Placebo is one of the flatterers and lickspittles that satirists attack so often. Being a 'court man' *par excellence*, and lackey to 'lordes of ful heigh estat' (1492 and 1495), he has no advice to give, he just serves Jnauary's will and pleasure. Justinus, his opposite, is in his way equally limited, because though he is inherently correct he lacks the social, persuasive powers of the good counsellor — Melibee's wife will be an example of that.

January, ill-served by his council, and ill-intentioned in any case, makes his choice. His surveying mind is like a mirror in a market place (1580–7) — familiar terrain for a merchant to purchase a wife.[56] Whatever is in his mind, his choice is given all the linguistic appurtenaunces of the lovely heroine:

> Hir fresshe beautee and hir age tendre,
> Hir myddel smal, hire armes longe and sklendre,
> Hir wise governaunce, hir gentillese,
> Hir wommanly berynge, and hire sadnesse.
>
> (1601–4)

But neither January nor market places can be trusted as a source for stock of this kind. The real nature of the marriage is underlined by the narrator in a way quite distant from this romance perfection:

> I trowe it were to longe yow to tarie,
> If I yow tolde of every scrit and bond
> By which that she was feffed in his lond
>
> (1696–8)

Some fine and apparently unironic language does appear: the marriage is briefly grand through Venus and her 'fyrbrond' (1727), but silence is imposed on that high style of a valued nobility, and the reason is slipped in like an ironic knife:

> Whan tendre youthe hath wedded stoupyng age,
> Ther is swich myrthe that it may nat be writen.

(1738–9)

Conflict is now developed in a dynamic complex of literary tradition and disturbing bathos. The marriage ceremony follows, and splendid poetry with it:

> Parfourned hath the sonne his ark diurne;
> No lenger may the body of hym sojurne
> On th'orisonte, as in that latitude.

(1795–7)

But these fine images and splendid works, stressed in rhyme, are only leading to a night of grisly marital details, given in truly churlish close-up:

> And Januarie hath faste in armes take
> His fresshe May, his paradys, his make.
> He lulleth hire, he kisseth hire ful ofte;
> With thikke brustles of his berd unsofte,
> Lyk to the skyn of houndfyssh, sharp as brere

(1821–6)

He is happy, if May is not. The image is driven home with a stunning picture of aged folly:

> He was al coltissh, ful of ragerye,
> And ful of jargon as a flekked pye.
> The slakke skyn about his nekke shaketh
> Whil that he sang, so chaunteth he and craketh.

(1847–50)

Such a marriage only deserves to go wrong, and its destruction is already in process; Damian loves May, May will reciprocate. Both of them do so in the correct language of *fin amor*, 'service' from the man and 'mercy' from the woman. May in fact is given again the line that expressed Theseus's noble 'pitee' (1986) but the whole process of letters thrust under pillows, hand-wringing and privy reading makes this as grotesquely inappropriate as

January's own use of the Song of Solomon (2138–48).

January's treatment of Damian is, however, admirable. He is concerned about the pretended sickness and speaks with genuine feeling (1906–15). The relationship is degraded from Damian's side, not January's. This has led humanist critics to feel sympathy for January, but they miss the point. The infidelity of the squire is another aspect of the acquisitive relations in this tale and to create that January must play a lord's part, however briefly.

Otherwise, January continues his possessive life, making a private garden with lock and key; keys become important in this tale, and they are symbols of the mercantile life, with things to lock away in privacy. But even though he keeps his hands on her like a purse (2091) and exercises her in a locked garden like a pet, the wife escapes. The husband, blind to so much that he should see, including the role of a calm old man, is tricked through the well-known motif of the lovers in the tree. But this is not merely a fabliau, enacting the ways in which people push and pull each other about in their individualist desires. This tale also moves on a theorized level, through its style, its narrator and its implication of social worlds. As in the Knight's tale this level of analysis is strengthened and clarified by the use of symbolic allegory. Pluto and Proserpine also use this garden, and as they discuss the husband/wife conflict Proserpine speaks up for the feminine position, asserting that while men may have Pluto's power and authority, women will have a competent response. Within the shadow of patriarchy there will be a sort of feminine liberty.

The story moves to its memorable conclusion with fabliau clarity and brevity – ' "Strugle!" quod he, "ye algate in it went"!' (2376) – and with all the tricky plotting of that realistic world. January thinks May is pregnant because of her interest in fruit, she persuades him she has saved him from blindness and his returning sight was mistaken. The comedy is without healing or vital force, more like the Reeve's tale than the Miller's. Where the fabliau world of the churls dispensed rough justice to men at least, here no one is harmed. The world of commodities and deceptions, the inauthentic world of merchants and selfish lords continues, and May even gives January hopes of reproduction, though that too may be inauthentic — like late medieval feudalism, illusionary or at best bastardized.

It maybe no accident that the Squire's tale follows the first tale which features a squire. The 'curteis and lowely' character of the Knight's Squire seems a conservative answer to the destructive discourtesy and hypocritical humility of January's Damian, just as the Clerk re-established clerical and masculine poise after the challenges posed through Friar and Wife.

At the outset the Squire establishes the existence of chivalric values like those imputed to his father: Cambuskan is

> . . . hardy, wys, and riche,
> And pitous and just, alwey yliche;
> Sooth of his word, benigne and honurable;
>
> (19–21)

The hero's knightliness is a pleasant change from January's crabbed greed, but this does not mean Cambuskan is not also rich and powerful. In the succeeding lines the absolute autocracy of the king is stressed — the possessive pronoun 'his' recurs throughout the passage detailing his unruffled splendour (45–78).

The development of the Squire's narrative establishes two major sequences before it breaks off. A horse of brass arrives at Cambuskan's court and an elaborate love story about birds is begun. These two threads would apparently have merged in a complicated narrative, but when he is two lines into it the Squire comes to a sudden end. Some critics have thought he is meant to be interrupted, as two pilgrims definitely are (Chaucer in 'Sir Thopas', and the Monk) and as perhaps the Cook was meant to be (p. 95). Others have thought Chaucer ran out of energy for a fairly fantastic story, just as he did with *Anelida and Arcite*, which bears some resemblance to the Squire's tale in its high-style emotional intricacy.

Whatever the unrecoverable authorial intention, as it stands the text works powerfully, because the Squire himself, the actual feudal youth, is an ineffectual ideologue for his own status, and offers no more than a brief and florid cultural diversion, a literary equivalent of his embroidered vest. It is through the Franklin that the text deals fully and strongly with problems about faithless squires and threats to aristocratic life and provides a fuller ideological answer to the types of disorder, familial and social, that have been raised in this long sequence of powerfully imagined responses to contemporary conflict.

Arrivisme, with its wish for cultural respectability, is the dominant motif of this Franklin's reaction to the Squire in his headlink, and also of the Host's distinctly rude treatment of the Franklin. Marginal to the gentry as he evidently is (like most class ideologues), the Franklin is a basis for a tale which is one of the most thorough pieces of conservative secular ideology in the whole *Tales*. It appears to resolve two major threats to patriarchal aristocracy, already raised in this group of tales — loss of a wife to another man with the implied loss of property and honour, and the independent role of a woman; to this the Franklin's tale adds a wider and newer dimension, the threat felt to established order from financial power and from the new skills of professionally trained individuals — such as those of the group to which the Franklin is allotted, however much he looks and yearns towards the landed gentry.

The primary conflict which the tale represents is the threat to the noble husband that he will lose his even more noble wife to a younger man. The January/Damian drama is played out in a less ignoble context than that provided by the Merchant. Dorigen, like all romance heroines has considerable and real value and property. It is '*hire* castel', not Averagus's, to which she repairs, and Aurelius is '*hire* neghebor' (847 and 961). Unlike a wifely 'thing' such as May or Griselda, she has the feudal power to make a binding oath to bestow herself elsewhere.

As is the conventionalized pattern of romance, love is the medium of this threat. Conventions in literature realize and indeed shape automatic responses in life and through the early romances love is established as the respectable chivalric code for the acquisitive desires of cavalry — to obtain another man's wife is to control her property, which was in the first place the point of marrying her. The consistent motif of seeing the beloved, whether young woman or wife, framed in her castle window or doorway, exemplifies the implicit meaning of 'love' in these romances; the related mechanism by which *fin amor* approaches were the rationalization of seizure completes the dynamic character of the convention.

So the Averagus–Dorigen–Aurelius triangle is an essentially feudal problem. It shows how the social bonds of feudalism were vulnerable, being based on oaths alone — the only form of contract and a notoriously fragile one, hence the insistence on its strength in culture. The conflict itself is made possible by the demands of the noble life: Averagus is away fighting and so his wife and her oaths are vulnerable.

Aurelius is himself an entirely admirable figure of chivalry:

> Yong, strong, right vertuous, and riche, and wys,
> And wel biloved, and holden in greet prys.

(933–4)

Unlike Damian, he is not the lord's own squire, and this attractive free force shapes his threat in the fully courtly context of the garden of love, stated to be cultural, artificial, made with 'craft of mannes hand' (909). The apparent innocence and actual danger of the love game is asserted when Dorigen, after a firm rejection of her sudden lover in terms of wifely fidelity, then gives 'in pley' (988) a second answer from the cultural courtly game — the impossible task with which ladies kept at a distance an unwanted suitor.

So from the heart of chivalry emerges the sharp point of 'competitive assertiveness', Courtly game, rash oaths, these security systems of culture in fact produce the sorts of threat they are developed to contain. The threat is relished painfully when the lord himself returns to confront it. Averagus weeps as he says that one's word must be kept:

> Trouthe is the hyeste thyng that man may kepe

(1479)

But the ideological and resolving reward for his nobility is a total dissolution of the threat. Aurelius, presented with the honest wife of the honest lord, falls into threat-resolving line. Where before he spoke as the free and exciting lover and then as the archetypal deserted figure, he finally speaks in the quasi-legal language of Averagus himself. He returns Dorigen, like the possession she inherently is, to her lord and proprietor, using the language of property:

> Quyt every serement and every bond
> That ye han maad to me as heerbiforn.

(1534–5)

The ideological circle is closed; class solidarity is resumed; Averagus the absentee husband can resume his life of bliss, power and property.

But that would be a simple story, and Chaucer's historical imagination is more complex and more contemporary. The feudal drama is a structure through which other, more contemporary threats are exhibited and resolved. The first arises from the means of fulfilling the rash oaths.

Aurelius's name has depths. An Aurelius was the traditional founder of Orleans, and the university there used Aurelianus as its adjective like Oxoniensis or Cantabrigiensis. It is from that university that the effective resolution of the impossible oath derives, because Aurelius's brother remembers a scientist–magician from his student days. The power that Aurelius directs at the feudal stasis, then, is not simply that of love. Indeed that is very readily disposed of by Dorigen and he immediately collapses into a very full version of the failed lover as pricked (though not silent) balloon. That defuses his love threat, only for his force to be revived as the director of the assembled power of scholarship and magic — and that is a power which is hired for hard, and enormous, cash.

There is an underlying structure here, of conflict between a Celtic and a French power for Brittany, symbolized by the sovereign lady.[57] But Chaucer has redirected this Celtic drama to bear the forces of contemporary history, namely the conflict between a manorial world and an urban, educated, professional, cash-involved social formation. This conflict was very vivid in the period as lords and legal technicians jostled for dominance and landed magnates became involved in business and financial dealings to defend and extend their power in the new world.

This drama is developed and sharply focused when, after Aurelius rejoins in language and attitude the manorial party, he is himself deeply distressed by a cash debt. He has nobly given up the lady; he must now pay the bill or face feudal extinction:

> Myn heritage moot I nedes selle
> And been a beggere; heere may I nat dwelle
> And shamen al my kynrede in this place,
>
> (1563–5)

But the 'master' (as he is usually called, a name redolent of education, technical skill and social authority) falls into feudal line and waves away both his mastery and debt; he too can behave like a knight:

> But God forbede, for his blisful myght
> But if a clerk koude doon a gentil dede
> As wel as any of yow, it is no drede!
>
> (1610–12)

Still the Franklin's tale twists and resists consoling stasis. Just as the Aurelius-based resolution led to his drastic debt, the master's surrender to feudalism calls up the socially equivocal figure of the Franklin. The master's notional equality with knight and squire is picked up by the narrator; in asking 'Which was the mooste fre' (1622) he poses a question that can only bring into prominence again the class conflict the tale has explored, and only invite a free-ranging and disturbing discussion about 'gentillesse' which, in the Wife's tale, started off this long sequence of fictionally coded social inquiry. The Franklin's presence, head-link, final question and existence as a difficult combination of the landed and the skilled: these are all signs that the modern world is not as simple as feudal ideology would have it, that tensions and redefinitions of status and values are continuing in history and will continue in *The Canterbury Tales*.

There is more yet in this rich tale. A common modern reception of the story produces another character as a candidate for 'freedom': when students are asked to answer the Franklin's final question they often (and not only women) suggest that Dorigen, who has suffered so much and has never imposed her will on anyone, is the only truly generous figure. It is not merely a modern viewpoint or one educated by feminism. The shape of the tale gives her a striking prominence, only to contain it urgently at the end.

As with the Wife and Criseyde, Chaucer gives so much space and voice to Dorigen that her viewpoint claims attention. When she is first left alone by Averagus, her distress is expressed not in silent misery or irrational behaviour, but in a powerful and coherent statement questioning divine order, proclaiming by the language and poise of its opening that this is no marital 'thyng' speaking:

> Eterne God, that thurgh thy purveiaunce
> Ledest the world by certein governaunce,
> In ydel, as men seyn, ye no thyng make.

(865 7)

This speech questions the ultimate order of providence; such vigorous dissent is partly contained by her final reduction into a simple prayer for Averagus's safety and her abdication of the field of speculative theology to 'clerkis' — but her final rhyme, 'conclusion' and 'disputison' (889–90) only restates her potential

power as linguist and analyst. That threat has been foreclosed
(literally – before) when the narrator, in introducing her feeling,
has generalized it dismissively:

> For his absence wepeth she and siketh,
> As doon this noble wyves whan hem liketh

(817–18)

But the poem seems to strain against that archetypal containment of the wife. As Aurelius prances before her, the presentation
is from her viewpoint; as she rejects him his reactions to her are
observed: she and her words have authority. Just as she states
her wifely fidelity she does so as a powerful person. The text even
reaches into her imagination. In the Boccaccian source the rash
oath was merely to have a garden flower in winter. But Chaucer
replaces this image of feminine whimsy with one of deep concern
for a loved husband — as she comes in courtly 'pley' to the need
for an impossible task, the black rocks that threaten the returning
Averagus surface destructively in her mind (992–7).

Since she is so fully realized a figure, it is hardly surprising that
at the crisis of the 'rash oath' plot she should dominate the stage.
Nor that this dominance, in the context of overriding patriarchal
authority, should be contained. Faced with the performance of
the task, Dorigen is dramatically astonished:

> He taketh his leve and she astoned stood;
> In al hir face nas a drope of blood.
> She wende nevere han come in swich a trappe.

(1339–41)

The skilfully devitalized poetry creates a sentient woman. She
expounds her position lucidly and intelligently:

> 'Allas' quod she, 'that ever this sholde happe!
> For wende I never by possibilitee
> That swich a monstre or merveile myghte be!
> It is agayns the proces of nature.'

(1342–5)

The complaint that follows, like so many long Chaucerian
speeches, is a steady subliminal revelation and evaluation of the
speaker. Starting as a tragic creation of a woman in a dilemma,
facing death or dishonour, it continues too long and ends too
inconsequentially. The narrator's original dismissal of self-

indulgently emotive women is resurrected in the action to contain the force of this feminine viewpoint and the last two lines of the speech were a Chaucerian addition to emphasize this ideological containment (1455–6).

She has taken no action, for all her early intentions; brisk action is the mode of masculine authority, as Averagus reveals when he returns and establishes an essentially austere patriarchal control:

> . . . 'I yow forbede, up peyne of deeth,
> That nevere, whil thee lasteth lyf ne breeth,
> To no wight telle thou of this aventure –
> As I may best, I wol my wo endure, –
> Ne make no contenance of hevynesse,
> That folk of yow may demen harm or gesse.'
>
> (1481–6)

Resolution of the feudal threat comes from husbandly firmness, action, feeling and control, and concern for the external world of honour. The wife goes and comes, like a 'thing' at last.

This radical containment of the feminine position, related as it imaginatively is to the Wife's prologue and tale, is no more than a potent restatement of the position established in the opening sequence of the tale. Averagus offered to continue the lover's stance within the marriage, but insisted that this must be secret:

> Save that the name of soveraynetee
> That wolde he have for shame of his degree.
>
> (751–2)

This is not merely a private equality pretending to be publicly authoritarian; Dorigen, like the Wife and like the old woman of her tale, accepts a subservient position which the text itself approves:

> And therfore hath this wise, worthy knyght
> To lyve in ese, suffrance hire behight,
> And she to hym ful wisly gan to swere
> That nevere sholde ther be defaute in here.
>
> (787–90)

Modern critics who read this as a marriage of equals in equal partnership have imposed modern practices (or ideologies) of marriage onto a quite different statement. This is to be a medieval marriage, tempered with affection, but still recreating in its structure the male authority that is the final ideological standpoint of the Franklin's tale.

The tales told by Physician and Pardoner are firmly linked together by the Host, but neither has any overt connection to any other tale. In the best manuscripts they always follow the Franklin, and they do have inherent links with that and its predecessors in two ways. The doctor's tale realizes more familial problems, the Pardoner's raises through images of a corrupt church economic patterns that have been consistent topics in this sequence of tales.

Like other well-established members of the professional group (Man of Law, Clerk and, soon, the poet himself), Physician tells a classical moral story and deals conservatively with medieval social and familial tension. Virginius is presented as a knight

> Fulfild of honour and of worthynesse,
> And strong of freendes, and of greet richesse.

(3–4)

He is vulnerable not through his wife or sister-in-law, like earlier magnates, but through his daughter, as Melibee will be. The opening part of this short tale makes three statements in connection with this new familial problem, all of them are extremely conventional, and each statement has the ideological force that necessarily underlies conventions — or they would not *be* conventional.

First, 'nature's finest work', a common element in the description of a beautiful woman. Her special qualities are imputed to nature, not to the aristocratic advantages of good diet, leisure, grooming and artificial assistance to beauty. By being 'nature's finest work', after which the mould was broken, the woman has the curious mixture of general qualities and individual pre-eminence that were inherent in the feudal, and more usually masculine, structure of public honour achieved by private 'competitive assertiveness'.

The description of the girl acts out that pattern; her virtues are moral and ideal like any of the conservative figures from the general prologue:

> . . . after hir degree
> She spak, and alle hir wordes, moore and lesse
> Sownynge in vertu and in gentillesse.
>
> (52–4)

She should be made aware of her role as the passive vessel of female aristocracy, seen from a nervous masculine viewpoint:

> For al to soone may she lerne loore
> Of booldnesse, whan she woxen is a wyf.
>
> (70–1)

Anxiety about controlling an heiress and anxiety about the growth of a powerful person — she will be both in time — are condensed together, and the third section turns to those older women who actually mould the child in cases like this. The tale addresses those 'maistresses' (bearers of worrying power not unlike the 'master' of the Franklin's tale) who 'lordes doghtres han in governaunce' (72–3) and urges them to teach the children not to stray into vice and lose their innocence — that is, lose their malleability to the parental will (as the Paston women grew into troublesome independence).

The action of the story shows that even success in that area may still bring no lasting joy. There are other threats to daughters and to property. Virginia is desired by Apius, an evil magistrate; he sends a churl to frame a case against Virginius, insisting that she is not his daughter but his own serf. With Apius's judgement against him, Virginius decides on Virginia's death before his dishonour and sends her head to the judge. The people rise up in anger, Apius is imprisoned and commits suicide, the churl is also condemned, but then, on Virginius' plea, exiled.

This chilling story has links back to the Franklin's tale, where death rather than dishonour was suggested but averted. There too the disturbance came initially from within the noble class, but was activated by professional skills and non-aristocratic force. The churl is a more extreme threat than the master magician, but the threats are remarkably similar. The resolutions however, are radically different. All the Physician's tale offers is a scorched-earth policy towards the in-class disturbers and the associated social invaders. At base and in its social setting this is a grimly despairing tale about the position of the traditional aristocracy; the assistance of the 'people' against the intervening forces (263–

8) is only a final and distinctly optimistic piece of wish-fulfilment, like the Young England movement in the nineteenth century, which looked to a lord—peasant coalition against the bourgeoisie.

Delany has pointed out how Chaucer redirected this tale from the pattern found in other versions.[58] Virginius is raised in social status to be at least the equal of the vicious judge. The role of the 'people' is contracted: usually representing the plebeian republicanism of Rome or anti-tyrannical forces in the medieval city, now they are merely a blunt instrument to support an aristocrat. As a result of his changes, Chaucer realizes in a devitalized form (as Delany argued) the feudal fear of legalistic and churlish incursions against an allegedly natural aristocratic power. The conservative theme fails to invoke the artist's historical imagination and so the Physician's tale is radically different from its successor, which centres on a figure that symbolizes at its most potent in *The Canterbury Tales* the threat of cash-based acquisitive individualism.

The figure of the Pardoner demonstrates all the skills of the 'noble ecclesiaste,' as was mentioned in the general prologue. But that role is subverted; this Pardoner is based ultimately on a character from the *Roman de la Rose* called Faux Semblaunt, best translated not as 'False Seeming' but as 'Bogus Exterior' or 'Misleading Appearance'. Nowadays it seems quite familiar to encounter a character whose bogus exterior masks an inner drive. This after all is the bourgeois idea of personality — a false social mask to conceal the real inner person. Modern terms like personality, persona, image, projection, medium, above all id, ego and superego — they ideologically produce this idea of what people essentially are.⏐

The medieval idea of the person (ontology) depended on a quite different, indeed reverse, notion, namely that people were primarily social and only in aberrance or in transition would be individual — the plot of romance, showing the lonely knight riding through imaginary wastelands to new social scenes of triumph, acts out the drama vividly. So for a character to be 'False' in his 'Exterior' is to subvert the existing order, it is a revolutionary notion of personality, not a ratification of the bourgeois concept of the person. This subversion and its socio-economic bases have been seen through the regular religious figures and the Summoner; it is radically extended through the Pardoner. He represents a worst case, a limit-searching study, of aggressive and acquisitive individualism; the disruptive force derives from the private use of the authentic skills of an officially authorized and public office.

Evil, self-aware, devoted only to pleasure and financial gain, the individual Pardoner floats free of any social or ethical nexus. Through his prologue he steadily separates himself from any connections. 'Bulles of popes and of cardynales' are shown (342), but they are evidently false; his relics themselves are exhibited, and his following spiel shows them to be ludicrous and only directed to bring in money — in themselves nothing but a 'gaude', a joke (389), or 'false japes' (394). This radically private figure cares nothing for the people he mocks, whether they go to hell or their children die of hunger (405–6, 450–1); but he cares for himself, taking sharp and financially oriented vengeance on those who critize him (412–422). He is not even linked to the cosmology by the paradox of doing good through evil: the possibility is raised three times, but he consistently denies that he suffers the pain that devils endured from only doing good (403–4, 423–34, 459–60); the notion has already been dramatized in the Friar's tale (1482–1500). The Pardoner's whole significance comes down to private, sensual interest.

But that, like all individualism, is itself a social and historical phenomenon. By description in his tale, the Pardoner is an archetype of the newly acquisitive individual, and Chaucer's historical imagination links him more strongly than any other pilgrim with the new world of cash and privatized social relations. It is coin he is after. He builds up the names of coins as a climax – 'pens, or elles grotes' (376), 'offre' (386) and, in his summary of his trade, a 'hundred mark' a year (390).

The Pardoner is Chaucer's most cash-obsessed pilgrim. Names of coins only appear thirty-one times in all of Chaucer's poetry, and twelve of the occurrences are here (five others are in the Friar's tale, a less emphatic version of this pattern). He mentions pence, groats, marks, florins, nobles, sterlings, referring to 'every kind of coin minted in England during the fourteenth century'.[59]

It is not only a matter of references. The structure of his sermon puts cash itself in the foreground; the 'tresor' that the three rioters find is a heap of splendid gleaming coins, not the mass of precious objects that would be a genuine old-world hoard, the sort of thing that feudal lords and epic kings kept to be dispensed to favourites and visitors. This is a merchant's capital resource, a bank for the new economic world:

Of floryns fyne of gold ycoyned round
Wel ny an eighte busshels

(770–1)

This pardoner combines the two elements which were necessary for capitalist take-off. First he is mobile, in wide-ranging carrying trade, moving through the country all the time, making enormous profit through the difference between the inherent value of his goods and services and the price he is able to obtain for them. The fact that the surplus value that is his profit is generated by people's faith and his own persuasion only stresses the subversion of Christian conservative values, and makes seem more terrible the mercantilism on which his meaning rests.

The second element in capitalism's take-off, according to Marx and modern theorists, is the formation of a pool of profit for reinvestment and conspicuous use. Through his own practices and the image of the 'tresor', the Pardoner's tale absorbs this as well. He is much more a figure of the new economic world than other disorderly characters: the Wife of Bath, though a small business figure, is involved in primitive manufacturing, firmly positioned by Marx on the feudal side of the great historical division between modes of production; the other businessmen, whether Miller, Burgess, Lawyer or Doctor, are all part of the urban version of manorial economy. This economy does not (in spite of many assertions, including some by some Marxists) belong with capital development, because its operations lack either or both of mobility and capital formation.[60]

One other feature of the tale belongs to this range of socioeconomic insights. It occurs in the world of the plague, and economic historians agree that the rapid development of a cash economy and new social relations in the later fourteenth century in Britain was, in part, caused by the high death rate in the mid-century which made labour scarce and disrupted traditional patterns of duty and inheritance across the country.[61]

Throughout the first part of the tale, the Pardoner gives in detail a softening-up harangue. Critics have excitedly praised the vivid orality of the performance, but have not noted enough how it subversively stresses the senses and the individual who epitomizes their regime. In performance, which this tale demands more than most, the following passage makes dramatic, vital and even authoritative, the world of the private drives and so calls up its final — and at this point feeble — rejection:

The apostel wepyng seith ful pitously
'Ther walken manye of whiche yow toold have I —
I seye it now, wepyng, with pitous voys —
That they been enemys of Cristes croys,
Of whiche the ende is deeth, wombe is hir god!'
O wombe! O bely! O stynkyng cod,
Fulfilled of dong and of corrupcioun!
At either ende of thee foul is the soun.
How greet labour and cost is thee to fynde!
This cookes, how they stampe, and streyne, and grynde
And turnen substaunce into accident,
To fulfille al thy likerous talent!
Out of the harde bones knokke they
The mary, for they caste noght awey
That may go thurgh the golet softe and swoote
Of spicerie of leef, and bark, and roote
Shal been his sauce ymaked by delit,
To make him yet a newer appetit.
But certes, he that haunteth swiche delices
Is deed, whil that he lyveth in tho vices.

(529–48)

Here, in the opening traditional statement, the speaker privileges himself as a new apostle, and as the passage moves relishingly and salivatingly through its physical creation from farting and cooking to swallowing; the new gospel of conspicuous consumption and personal physical enjoyment is enacted with stunning impact.

Gaming and swearing receive realizations only a little less dramatic and, against them as preparation, the stark tale operates. Its mode and structure are a powerfully formative part of the developing challenge to authority, secular and religious. Having inverted the rhetoric of the church, this Pardoner speaks in the plain, detailed style of the fabliau; his actual story crackles along with action, reaction, motive and explanation, creating the personal, close-up world of self-realization, and its own pacing (static drama in the harangue, mobile headlong velocity in the story) enacts in itself the sense of an old world succumbing to a modern whirlwind.

The sheer dynamism of the Pardoner's self-creation, to be compared with the surroundings of rumour and the violent upsurge of the lower birds, establishes a position of such power and such threat that it calls up multiple ideological containments. First there is the story's own self-destruction, that the 'rioters' die in their quest; and that the Pardoner himself is involved in that autonomous holocaust is the message of his frequent references to avarice as his own sin. But the end of the tale is not content to leave it there, in mere self-contradiction. The Pardoner makes, as part of his performance, a closing prayer which leads on to a statement in his own voice of his own dishonesty:

> And lo, sires, thus I preche.
> And Jhesu Crist, that is our soules leche
> So graunte yow his pardoun to receyve,
> For that is best; I wol yow nat deceyve.

> (915–18)

Critics from Kittredge onwards who recreate *The Canterbury Tales* as a humanist quasi-novel have fretted mightily over this. Is it a genuine revulsion of feeling, a character finally seeing the ethical light like Tom Jones? Or is it a final act of the master manipulator, softening up his pilgrim audience for the following spiel as he did his imaginary and regular audience for prologue and his tale? To see the tales as a whole — as structures which realize through typical figures the forces of the contemporary world — is the way to dissolve the problem. At the end of the tale the whole positioning of the Pardoner is recreated so that the disruptive figure can be judged and contained.

First the ideal situation is stated; the often quoted lines (915–18) act as Knight, Parson and Plowman act in the general prologue. Then the Pardoner's own role-reversal is dramatized as, like the self-seeking figures in the general prologue, he imposes his private interests through the skills of his role. He offers relics and pardon to the pilgrims with an appropriate persuasion:

> It is a honour to everich that is heer
> That ye mowe have a suffisant pardoneer
> T'assoile yow, in contree as ye ryde,
> For aventures whiche that may bityde.

> (931–4)

The fact that this is less convincing and less potent than what has gone before does not mean he is tongue-in-cheek here; it means he can more easily be dismissed, and the Host, as usual, performs the judging function with an anger which expresses the view of conservative society towards this Pardoner and his threat.

But the terms of the Host's dismissal are only initially Christian:

> 'Nay nay,' quod he, 'Thanne have I Cristes curs!'
>
> (946)

He goes on to raise unmistakably the matter of the Pardoner's bizarre sexuality − this is the ground on which the bogus relics are rejected:

> But, by the croys which that seint Eleyne fond,
> I wolde I hadde thy coillons in myn hond
> In stide of relikes or of seintuarie.
> Lat kutte hem of, I wol thee helpe hem carie;
> They shul be shryned in an hogges toord!
>
> (951–5)

The Host acts as one foul-mouthed churl grappling with another, like Miller and Reeve, and so mutually dissipating their threat. He also acts as the voice of normative judgements and points irresistibly back to the all-embracing containment of the Pardoner, set up in the general prologue. His sexuality is bizarre; whatever the details might be, he is not fully masculine, he cannot have children − that is, history and the future cannot, must not, belong to his kind.

The homosexuality of the pardoner is not an embarrassingly illiberal attitude on Chaucer's part − though it may have that impact in modern re-readings of the tale. It is a code for containment of the most disturbing figure of all; and, interestingly, the motif is familiar in the context of cash relations. Discussions of the very disturbing structure of cash profit, usury or, as Langland calls it, 'meed', frequently say that money itself is sterile and cannot reproduce itself. Chaucer has projected a commonplace into high, even violent, ideological drama, realizing through his fiction some of the most intimate and far reaching features of his socioeconomic world.

So, a strained peace falls; and its manipulation into being raises one last twist of the historical imagination. The Knight, that figure of the past and searcher for order among chaos, makes Host and Pardoner kiss: the embrace of urban business and radical individualism is both a conventional conclusion with little conviction and a probing glimpse of the future already developing, a telling example of the artist's power both to capture and to judge history in formation.

This extreme tale comes to a dramatic and ambivalent ending, so summing up the extraordinary and disturbing power of this long and unmatched sequence of tales from Wife of Bath through to Pardoner. The third and final sequence which follows them is a less searching and volatile set of tales, which moves steadily towards a conservative and Christian stasis. That containment is apparently called up by the rich, subtle and inherently radical force of the second sequence.

IV   From the Shipman's tale to the Retractions: 'Taketh the fruyt, and lat the chaf be stille'

The tales from Shipman to Nun's Priest form the longest finished sequence in the whole *Canterbury Tales*. After the complex tension of the previous tales, those gathered here seem a little simplistic; they tend to develop only one idea in a static context, lacking the sociohistorical dynamics that were created from Wife of Bath through to Pardoner. There are many signs in the Shipman to Nun's Priest group of containment being applied to those historical and disruptive forces. They are not forgotten, but they are realized in a less far-reaching and more easily negatived way. The same pattern, as will be argued towards the end of this section, is also found in the last four tales, from Second Nun to Parson, though here the forces of disruption are raised only to be rejected in that final sequence of increasingly overt conservatism, both secular and religious.

The tale allotted to a Shipman both exposes and affirms mercantile values, but does it in a way more lifeless and more easily rejected than earlier realizations of that force; the tale is much closer to the French fabliau, with its aristocracy-reassuring role. The opening lines deal with the double character of a merchant, but find no problem in treating him and his admirers ironically, saying he 'riche was, for which men helde hym wys' (2). The voice knows and judges merchants surely, as neither the general prologue nor the Merchant's tale found the ability to do. Whose voice this might be is less certain. It has long been assumed that, as lines 11–19 are spoken by a woman, the passage and so the tale were drafted for the Wife of Bath. That seems suitable to the fabliau genre, the concern with sex and money and the vigorous final joking about 'taillynge' — tallying money and playing with your (or someone else's) tail. No other woman seems a likely teller — not even the heights of critical fancy have yet, apparently, excavated one of the burgesses' wives for the role.

Chaucer apparently decided in his process of rethinking and reworking the *Tales* that he could produce something which projected the figure of the Wife both as a woman and a businesswoman more strongly and more subtly, and with more sociohistorical power. Left with a tale to allocate, he stayed within the professional group for a teller to whom the mercantile material was natural and for whom the boisterous tone also seemed suitable, but the position of a Shipman is not itself explored or projected in any way.

The essence of the story is that sexuality and money are bound up together. The monk more or less buys the wife; the husband regains lustiness when his profits mount; the wife says of her debt:

I am youre wyf; score it upon my taille,

(416)

and then develops the metaphor of mercantile sexuality:

Ye shal my joly body have to wedde;
By God, I wol not paye yow but abedde.

(423–4)

This commercialization of human relations has been generally apparent, but critics have not seen that the whole tale appears to comprehend and realize intimately the commodity-based social relations of the capital world.

It is from the manorial position that this pattern is defined: the merchant is seen as 'noble' (20) and is said to behave 'gentilly' (281), but in fact he is not in any way aristocratic or involved in feudal social relations. In order to be his business self he must be private (85) and the action makes it clear, as he does, that business practice and the public feasting of the noble world are at odds — this is the impact of the lively dialogue from 208–38.

The social life he avoids is with a monk who is said to be his 'cousin' from the same village. Both figures are offered a communality which both eschew – the merchant in his counting house, the monk by denying it when he too wants to make a profit, financial and sexual (149). The relationship, denied at the kin and social level, obviously exists at the behavioural level, as cozenage not cousinage (suggested in 409). The merchant and monk are different archetypes of the same formation; once more, merchant and cleric are fatefully related — the Reeve's tale opened with such a statement about a miller and a parson, the Pardoner's, Summoner's and Friar's tales acted out in practice that convergence.

The emphasis of the tale is heavily on private, mercantile and competitive dealing; merchant and monk are only seen to dine together in public for four lines (251–4) before they return to their shared privacy to strike a bargain that the self-deluding merchant thinks is noble and the monk intends to be profitable. The merchant's practices are presented with detail and relish; his whole self-consciousness is financial, so that his personal progress is climaxed when

> . . . hoom he goth, murie as a papejay,
> For wel he knew he stood in swich array
> That nedes moste he wynne in that viage
> A thousand frankes aboven al his costage.
>
> (369–72)

As in the Pardoner's tale, mobility and massive profit come together, the workings of the mercantile world depend on cunning and deception and assume that private acquisitiveness is the purpose of life and the pleasure of living. Yet here there is no strong negative treatment of the practices as there was in the rhetorically and religiously subversive Pardoner; rather, each of the characters is bruised but resilient, a world is created where infidelity is normal and where sin does not exist, whether in religious or humanist terms — this is the world of fetishized commodities that Marx outlined.[62]

If that seems a merely reflective and uninvestigative level for a tale, such relative simplicity of mode and tone is to some degree the pattern of this entire group and is quite different from the impact of the preceding tales. Complete as it is, the group is not as rich in conflict as the earlier ones; it is rather a sequence where positions are defined specifically and in a contained way, not seen as the producers and products of dialectic social conflict. There is a modal and imaginative simplification from the beginning of this group that basically lasts to the end of the *Canterbury Tales*, and when there is complexity in this group it tends itself to promote quietism, as in the last tale, told by the Nun's Priest.

If the Shipman's tale shows woman, and man as well, being mercantilized, a quite different reduction of feminine potential is set out through the Prioress's tale. Positioned at a high social level by the Host's conditional and subjunctive language to her (446–50), she moves into a short, elegant tale. As she starts, the religious note is strong and distinctly graceful, performed for the first time in the *Canterbury Tales* in the complex form of rhyme royal. Elevated in language and rhetorical motifs, complex in syntax and metrical movement, this is an authentic religious high style. The speaker, however, says of herself that 'My konnyng is so wayk' that she is 'as a child of twelf month oold, or less' (481 and 484). That is a proper Christian self-abnegation, but it may be more. As the tale opens not only does its style simplify radically, its topic also becomes that of a very small child.

Criticism has raised two separate but related problems in interpreting this version of the familiar child-martyr story. First, does Chaucer mean the tale to be unacceptably anti-semitic? The case has been made vigorously by Richard Schoeck, both from the implications of the text and from contemporary statements deploring savage treatment of Jews and attitudes condoning it. The opposite position has been taken in a survey of the matter by Florence Ridley.[63] The dominant opinion is that Schoeck uses rather rare examples to buttress a case built more on modern attitudes than medieval ones. Unless more discoveries are made about Jews and attitudes to them in Chaucer's Europe, the case must rest substantially on the text itself, and there it seems that the emphasis is not on the race that murdered and suffered terribly in return, but rather on the position of the story-teller.

So the racist question shades into the second critical problem about the tale: is it representing a limited sentimental response to religion, filling out the meaning of this Prioress in the general prologue, or is the tale a fit and proper Christian statement, of a particular sort? Two medievalists have spoken against an 'ironic' reading of the tale; Russell and Hirsh both see it as related positively to the mass for Holy Innocents' Day, an uncriticized example of affective religion.[64] Neither scholar is readily to be rejected, but both may have weighed the context they know so well more heavily than the text itself.

To read the tale, and especially to read it aloud, makes prominent the 'litel' character of the martyr, repeated through lines like 'This litel child, his litel book lernynge' (516) and culminating in 'his litel body sweete' (682). The figures of the 'mice' and 'smale houndes' seem to be invoked — this Prioress's 'conscience' was devoted to them. The reference to the speaker as a 'twelf month child or less' appears not innocent in this context, and her own language has been described as having a 'school-child's syntax'.[65]

The action of the tale itself seems to be distinctly sensational (that dialectic partner of sentimentality) with the horror of the crime stressed deeply:

> I seye that in a wardrobe they hym threwe
> Where as thise Jewes purgen hire entraille.
>
> (572–3)

And the last lines seem to emphasize mercy in an odd way: the Prioress finally prays

> That, of his mercy, God so merciable
> On us his grete mercy multiplie,
>
> (688–9)

The whole concept of mercy has not been considered before, especially not for the criminals and their compatriots; the use of the word again seems related to its deliberate downgrading in the general prologue.

There is enough in the theme and form of the text to make it doubtful that Chaucer means this Prioress to be an entirely admirable figure, and that seems more clearly the case after the tale of her assistant, the Second Nun, (see pp. 145–7). The Prioress's tale is an effective development of the general prologue, but in being no more than that, it is a good deal less wide-ranging and searching, especially in a sociohistorical way, than most of the previous tales.

If the Prioress's tale is a partial parody of the child-martyr story, the following tale is wholly a literary parody, one of the finest in the English language. Like the best of the genre, 'Sir Thopas' is funny in its own right, then more deeply funny in its revaluation of the mode it mocks. The jokes of content are clear even to those who know no earlier English romances. That bijou name for a knight, Thopas, is plainly unsuitable; the intrinsic comedy of his location, unaristocratic Flanders, is made evident by the plodding pomp of the line 'At Poperyng, in the place' (720); the unseemly and over-genteel pallor of this unimpressive knight is the climax of the simile: 'Whit was his face as payndemayn' (725) and this doughy doughtiness prepares for the crashing bathos of the stanza's end: 'He hadde a semely nose' (729).

The thematic jokes are themselves stressed by the poetic form, and other purely formal jokes are made: the feeble use of a line-filler to find the second rhyme in 'verrayment' (713) is even weaker than the preceding rhyme, 'in good entent' (712). Another strained word provides a rhyme in 'gent' (715) and stanza two (718 and 722) commits the solecism of using exactly the same word in rhyme without the elegant variation of *rime riche* (in which the word sounds the same but is etymologically different).

So Chaucer catches on the cruel point of parody both the amiable banality of middle-of-the-road romance and also its blurred, lame technique: 'Sir Thopas' shows a world of understanding of the attitudes, motifs and language of the English romances.[66] But this type of simple and direct narrative in a restricted linguistic code is far from Chaucer's chosen European, sophisticated mode of literary production; the parody is amusing but it is also used to incite the Host's attack on the author and on poetry. He states:

> Thou dost noght elles but despendest tyme.
> Sire, at o word, thou shalt no lenger ryme.

> (931–2)

Chaucer accepts the command. Perhaps he accepts the accusation about time-wasting as well.

This moment should be reconsidered when the *Tales* are finished, and the Retractions have been pondered. In the Host's foul-mouthed and intemperate bullying, there seems to be the beginning of a steady movement of withdrawal from art, poetry, the subtle voice, the secular arts. The first prose tale, told by Chaucer and much more important than most critics have realized, seems to endorse in its form the idea that poetry has limited value. This withdrawal is then steadily supported by direct and indirect statement, until the second and overtly Christian prose sequence finally dominates the *Tales*.

The tale of Melibee has not often been read, certainly not often

with enthusiasm. Some feel it is deliberately dull art,[67] but its
startling quality is that it does talk about Chaucer's own period,
in as direct a way as he ever manages. Seen in terms of the late
fourteenth century and in the aftermath of the Peasants' Revolt,
the tale of Melibee, the tale that is presented as a proper
alternative to poetry, is a thoughtful piece of political persuasion
aimed at, and ultimately aimed to help, the powerful in England
in the 1380s.

Even those scholars who have looked for historical meaning of
this tale seem to have missed its drift. Stilwell connected it with
Richard II's foreign policy, perhaps to the strain between
Richard and the Duke of Lancaster. Hotson related it to John of
Gaunt's problems in Castile. Howard perceived it as 'an address
the court' but finds no specific sociopolitical relevance; Lawrence
sensed 'the evils of war and the perversion of justice' behind the
tale, and Aers described it as 'Chaucer's own critique of
militarism and war'.[68]

The tale is more politically detailed and effective than these
critics suggest. Melibee is a rich man, with an only daughter.
Vulnerability seems consistently the meaning of this state, and he
has been outraged. His daughter was severely wounded when his
house was broken into by his 'olde foes' (970). The whole tale
discusses and establishes his response to this. Like the manorial
figure he is, he calls up a council of friends and relatives. The
advice is confusingly various — doctors say they will heal the
daughter, lawyers advise cautious defence, young men want some
action, the troublemakers urge revenge; a wise old man insists on
the problems of war, but is shouted down.

An allegorical dimension exists in the tale: the daughter is
named Sophia, or Wisdom, the wife is Prudence and 'Melibee' is
explained as rich with the honey of wealth (1410). As in the
dream poems and the Knight's tale, through allegory comes
contemporary analysis. The assault on Melibee's house and the
planned responses of various sorts are all strongly related to the
experiences and attitudes of the propertied classes in the
immediate aftermath of the Peasants' Revolt. The riot of contrary
advice that opens the story leaves Melibee puzzled. Prudence
settles his problems about his counsellors, and when he asks how
he can separate good people from bad without taking vengeance,
she explains the role of law (1430), a statement at once allegorical
and political.

The most potent sequence follows Melibee's boasting about his power, authority and riches (1575). Prudence harangues him on the proper practices in connection with wealth, how to obtain it without too much greed or haste and too much harm to others, how to use riches generously for the common good, how to defer to God through the enjoyment and accumulation of riches. It is a programme for the successful control of wealth and power, given in some detail and with some strictures on common bad practices.

Finally, Prudence advises Melibee on how to act in his present distress. He is all for seizing his enemies' goods and forcing them into exile; she persuades him to accept their penitence, give pardon and secure both peace and his own augmented honour. So a programme for reform of the use of riches is attached to the whole conservative projection of the future. The last word is distinct Christian support for this flexible conservatism as Melibee receives his enemies into his grace and reminds them briefly of that other lord, before whose grace everyone is equal (1880–7).

At the core of *The Canterbury Tales* stands this serious and thoughtful address to the powerful on how to save their power. This is the author's second, considered story, and it comes in the centre of the longest finished group of tales. In passing it over as dull, in seeing it lightly as a boring joke, or in finding in it only the spiritual levels of allegory, most Chaucerians have failed to see the signals that point clearly to the political importance of this tale.

The Host as usual only reacts in crass individualist terms, and the next pilgrim's response is equally inadequate. The Monk's series of gloomy disasters pales against the positive conservatism of Dame Prudence. His definition of tragedy (1973–7) makes it clear that it is an awkward and mechanical piece of memory-work, with its jingling rhymes and clumsily Latinate utterance in 'to seyn' and 'make us memorie' (1973–4). Worse still, he apologizes in case it is not accurate and assures the audience that he will tell his tragedies in any order, as they 'cometh unto my remembrance' (1989).

What follows is thematically a development of the point made so far entirely by literary form. All the Monk can offer is a set of sensational accounts of the fall of great men and women, with simple explanatory tags that the blame should fall on Fortune, the treachery of relatives or allies, or, when the characters are biblical, on sin in the fallen person. The old-fashioned Benedictine tradition of monastic history is exposed — somewhat unfairly — in its most naïve and reductive form.

One of the short lives is typical enough:

> O worthy Petro, kyng of Cipre, also
> That Alisandre wan by heigh maistrie,
> Ful many an hethen wroghtestow ful wo,
> Of which thyne owene liges hadde envie,
> And for no thyng but for thy chivalrie
> They in thy bed han slayn thee by the morwe.
> Thus kan Fortune hir wheel governe and gye,
> And out of joye brynge men to sorwe.
>
> (2391–8)

Envy and misfortune are causes of disaster that leave no blame with the victim; Prudence was both more incisive and more practical. She had a lot to say about the misuse of riches, and she also shaped a response to the negative experiences of the powerful in the period. After seventeen of these little tragedies, the Knight has heard enough — he would like to hear about stories of social and financial success and upwards movement,

> As whan a man hath been in povre estaat
> And clymbeth up and wexeth fortunat
> And there abideth in prosperitee.
>
> (2775–7)

Such lives do not exist in the *Tales*, though they were well known in late medieval life, like those of the powerful Archbishop Wykeham and Sir John Hawkwood the great captain, apart from men of Chaucer's acquaintance who rose through business like Nicholas Brembre or Gilbert Maghfeld. Social innovation of that sort is merely an undeveloped mention in a poem which is now increasingly conservative in politics and in attitudes to learning and analysis. Having dismissed old-style scholarship as powerless to comprehend and respond to disorders, past and present, the text moves on in the next tale to satirize and ultimately discard as equally useless the complexities of modern scholarship.

The Nun's Priest is described briefly, and without apparent irony, as 'This sweete preest, this goodly man, sir John' (2820). His tale is sweet and goodly in a number of ways — comic, finely imagined, delicately satirical, but it is finally 'sweete' and 'goodly' in the most simple, devout and conservative of senses.

The tale is set among the lowest of all classes, with a poor rural widow. Friar and Clerk both mentioned the poor peasantry, but in neither case were they central as such. Those treatments had a certain residual sense of grievance in them and it is notable that the speakers who do deal with the truly poor are all clerics — and the Pardoner, who exploits this class most viciously of all, belongs dialectically in the same category. The range of the stories recognizes the contact between churchmen and the lowest social stratum, which led in some cases to clerical revolutionary leaders, liberation theologues of their period. But in the Nun's Priest's tale, the widow's life is offered as a model of quietism, a version of the patient and glad poverty that was a major ideological constraint on lower class disturbance in the period.

This long series of tales has consistently rejected various cultural forms as more or less invalid, only allowing the prose reasoning of Melibee to have any current validity. The Nun's Priest's tale brings this movement to a climax; it sports with, realizes and then discards the ultimate complexities of late fourteenth century thought, and at last advocates rural simplicity as a proper response. That deliberate reduction of focus ends this long group, and is the point from which the last four tales will develop a specifically Christian version of that rejection of the secular world, dismissing both its disorders and its human strivings for advancement and comprehension.

But the tale does not make that simplicity seem dull; on the other hand its brilliant comedy vivifies and so legitimizes its final conservatism. From the very beginning a mastery of poetic language works to make a series of subtle and negative points. The widow's life is described plainly in tones of black and white, for she 'In pacience led a ful symple lyf' (2826). The niceties of a sophisticated table and vocabulary are equally tasteless to her (2832–9). The result is a good life: her lack of 'repleccioun' is 'temperance' and in 'exercise and suffisaunce' she finds health and peace (2839).

This skilfully crafted opening gives the key to the tale as a complex process of realizing and rejecting sophisticated values.

This is created through a beast fable — a common conservative method, from Aesop to Orwell. The widow has a splendid cock called Chauntecleer and his famous description places him among the more splendid knights of romance:

> Lyk asure were his legges and his toon;
> His nayles whitter than the lylye flour
> And lyk the burned gold was his colour.

> (2862–4)

This heraldically described cock is a romantic hero:

> This gentil cok hadde in his governaunce
> Seven hennes for to doon all his pleasaunce

> (2865–6)

The fine language and the elegant measures of romance writing are raised only to be crashingly disrupted by their bathetic hen-house context: these ladies were, after all, both 'his sustres and his paramours' (2867).

The text moves on to another cultural topic, the theory of dreams — itself richly treated in Chaucer's own work. A debate follows between lord and lady or cock and hen, on the meaning of Chauntecleer's grim dream. She like any lady, is alarmed that her hero might be a coward and with the healing skills of the true princess (and fairy mistress too) she prescribes purgative herbs which occur in the farmyard — the language destroys the ladylike edifice as she also recommends him to: 'Pekke hem up right as they growe and ete hem in.' (2967). Chauntecleer in return is a hero of dream lore and dreams, arguing at great length for their validity, but relying on no more than vague analogues and unidentified authorities (2974–7). Having proved his case to his own satisfaction, he makes it plain that, like many scholars present and past, his own satisfaction is the point: he climbs down from the perch and starts his day, in spite of his proof that it will turn to evil. Pertclote's beauty gives courage to this farmyard chevalier:

> Ye been so scarlet reed aboute youre yen
> It maketh al my drede for to dyen;

> (3161–2)

As the tale moves into its action, the consistent use of scholarly digression in increasingly comic and devalued ways deepens the sense that the Chaucer who before the tale of Melibee accepted the ruling that he should 'ryme no moore' is here using his range of reference and his mastery of poetic tone to reject both reference and ultimately poetry itself. Chauntecleer reveals himself as being, like Chaucer, a fine astronomer (3187–97) and then grandly invites his beloved to listen to the birds sing, as befits a knightly hero. But evil is to come, with a cultural context wider than mere romance:

> But sodeynly hym fil a sorweful cas,
> For evere the latter ende of joye is wo.
> God woot that wordly joye is soone ago;
> And if a rethor koude faire endite,
> He in a cronycle saufly myghte it write
> As for a sovereyn notabilitee.

> (3204–9)

Many types of 'sovereyn notabilitee' are to be mocked — the pompous Latin phrase itself is allowed to sink through its own weight, like so much of what follows. First romance is derided:

> This storie is also trewe, I undertake,
> As is the book of Launcelot de Lake
> That wommen holde in ful greet reverence.

> (3211–13)

As the conservative wit closes in on the range of human intellectual endeavour, limiting responses to patience and peace of mind, any sense that women too might have a voice and position is also being rejected.

The deep and passionate late medieval debate on predestination is the next cultural item to be jettisoned; the presence of the fox in the cabbages becomes the occasion for learned consideration of free will and God's design, ruthlessly cut down by the narrator after it has been realized in authentic terms:

> My tale is of a cok, as ye may heere.

> (3252)

There follow minor thrusts at medieval scholarship on mermaids (3230–2), theory of contraries (3279–81), music (3291–2), rhetoric (3347–54) and the classics (3355–74); all of these are droll, but they are also rejections of the whole medieval enterprise of human learning, the industry which not only sustained the Christian church but also preserved and transmitted the culture of the classical age. To mock all this is to dismiss some of the finest achievements of the human spirit in that period; it is odd that those humanist critics who most admire and value those things today should find this anti-cultural tale so entertaining. The joke, the smile, are no more than the genial front for a cultural holocaust.

It is from this position of anti-cultural conservatism that Chaucer makes his one overt comment on the Peasants' Revolt, when he briefly and memorably realizes the din and chaos of the farmyard rescue of the cock:

> Certes, he Jakke Straw and his meynee
> Ne made never shoutes half so shrille
> What that they wolden any Flemyng kille,
> As thilke day was maad upon the fox.
>
> (3394–7)

The reference is to the attack on foreign merchants in London in the riot stage of the revolt. A particularly gruesome event is mentioned, one which was least related to the political meaning and anti-aristocratic tendency of the revolt. And the reference is made only in a simile as the story closes down to its domestic, farmyard conclusion. A set of multiple containments operate against this fragment of reality of 1381; the technique of the context is one of Chaucer's finest pieces of close-up realism, but it is now in so rigidly restrained a context, politically, socially, even intellectually, that the technique does not dramatize social conflict as it did in the first two major sections of the *Tales*, but merely presents a vignette of peasant simplicity and unthreatening normality — where 'pacience' and 'hertes suffisaunce' are imposed as the dominant values.

For the cock, the moral is keep your eyes open; but it is the fox's moral which is given in direct speech, given last and which seems to be woven into the developing conservatism of the tales:

> 'Nay', quod the fox, 'but God yeve hym meschaunce
> That is so undiscreet of governaunce
> That jangleth whan he sholde holde his pees.'
>
> (3433–5)

The fox's words seem to look forward to the Manciple's tale, and to the Retractions themselves. The priest insists that his tale has a meaning:

But ye that holden this tale a folye,
As of a fox, or of a cok and hen,
Taketh the moralite, goode men.
For seint Paul seith that al that writen is,
To oure doctrine it is ywrite, ywis;
Taketh the fruyt, and lat the chaf be stille.

(3438–43)

The technique of the tale has produced the notion that a whole range of literary and scholarly endeavour is no more than chaff; the fruit must lie back with the widow's limited diet and equally limited state — and peace — of mind. The peasantry and their revolt only appear in the *Canterbury Tales* when the disruptive forces that flourished in the first two sequences have been steadily contained through a satirical and limited group of tales. The stage that remains is the Christian conclusion.

The last four tales appear in three separate fragments, but the geographic details insist that they belong together just before the arrival at Canterbury, where the best manuscripts place them. The party has apparently left Ospringe, the usual overnight stop before Canterbury, at the beginning of the Canon's Yeoman's tale, which is linked in the narrative to the preceding Second Nun's tale. The Manciple's tale starts close to Harbledown, as the London road bobs over a fold in the downs and then dips into the Stour valley, where Canterbury stands and the Parson's tale begins.

In theme too this is a united group; varied as usual in tone and teller, it nevertheless directs its thrust towards a strong religious ending, the abandonment of secular values and even that of literature itself. The Second Nun's tale asserts straight, orthodox Christianity after the Nun's Priest has dismissed all other late medieval cultural practices. Her prologue uses the seven-line stanza that was employed by her senior, the Prioress. Here too, Mary is invoked, but in a context very different from that of the Prioress's fine church rhetoric and naïve awe. Here Mary is an active force of feminine good:

Thow Mayde and Mooder, doghter of thy Sone,
Thow welle of mercy, synful soules cure,
In whom that God for bountee chees to wone,
Thow humble, and heigh over every creature.

Thow noblest so ferforth our nature,
That no desdeyn the Makere hadde of kynde
His Sone in blood and flessh to clothe and wynde.

(36–42)

The tone is reverent, sensitive of religious paradox and mystery, but also deeply practical. In the same spirit, the nun says firmly:

And, for that feith is deed withouten werkis,
So for to werken yif me wit and space,

(64–5)

This is strongly opposed to the Prioress; here the issue is a busy religion first correcting the world and then turning its attention to the heavenly future. The story of St Cecilia is a strong and detailed narrative which lacks both the sentiment and the easy, almost facile, fluency of the Prioress's tale.

Cecilia marries, but has no intention of accepting in its own terms a secular condition: she wears a hairshirt under her bridal gown and soon enough persuades her husband and his brother to adopt both chastity and Christianity. All the tangles of the tales told from Wife through to Pardoner, enmeshed as they were in marital and social confusions, are side-stepped with one firm movement.

The saint's power takes her men quite beyond the secular world; they gladly go to execution, as does Maximus, the prefect's officer, who is converted by the behaviour of these saints and so beaten to death with a whip of lead. As so often in stories that reject mundane values, whether saints' lives or Gothic romances, physicality is relished in a bittersweet (or sado-masochistic) way. Cecilia sits in a bath of flames for two days without being affected; then a *coup de grace* is bungled and she spends three days with her neck cut in half; the Christians mop up her blood with sheets and she keeps on teaching until she is released in death.

That is the way of saints' legends and this is an unflinching and thoroughly developed one, deployed throughout in the stately confidence of the rhyme royal stanza, relishing its innate tendency to bring a summary in its final couplet — a feature largely avoided in the Prioress's tale. The firmness of the poetry and the rigour given to the saint are plain when she answers Almachius:

'Ye han bigonne youre questioun folily,'
Quod she, 'that wolden two answeres conclude
In o demande; ye axed lewedly.'
Almache answerde unto that similitude,
'Of whennes comth thyn | answeryng so rude?'
'Of whennes?' quod she, whan that she was freyned,
'Of conscience and of good feith unfeyned.'

(428–34)

For the first time in the whole *Tales*, the orthodox voice of Christianity is heard without apology, embarrassment or irony. The 'hertes suffisaunce' given as a simple secular positive in the Nun's Priest's tale is amplified in full Christian power in the tale told by that other unobtrusive servant of the showily ladylike Prioress. It is as if the lower orders in the church were now asserting truths forgotten by their superiors, a sort of clerical peasants' revolt of a kind very different from the political one, in fact directly opposed to it. This will be ratified and massively confirmed by the long, strong and final voice of that cleric who is of peasant stock, the Parson.

But before that, two others will speak, Canon's Yeoman and Manciple, the one a servant of the church, the other a lawyer's steward. From their subordinate positions, they expose first the ludicrous and diabolic activities of a gold-obsessed scholar cleric, and then state formally the final word on the risks involved in personal intervention both in human life and in literature.

The fact that Nun's Priest and Second Nun went undescribed in the general prologue suggests that their important role at the end indicates a change of plan in the whole poem, one matching the abandonment of the scheme to return to London. The Canon and his Yeoman are more strikingly innovative: they erupt into the story, joining the pilgrimage of their own will and in great haste. This does not suggest, as some critics have thought, that they are on the run from a confidence trick at Ospringe; rather they are a symbol of social incursion and, soon enough, of equally abrupt rejection. When the shifty canon hears his private deeds are being made public, he disappears (700–2): exposure dissolves his threat as it did not that of the previous corrupt churchmen.

The Canon's Yeoman's tale is effectively in three parts: a very long headlink, a full and confessional prologue somewhat like the

Pardoner's, a fairly short and not very dramatic tale about a typical alchemical con-man who happens to be a canon. The development of the frame at the expense of the story makes this seem likely to be a late tale, but it is also one which asserts personality and realism — and then shows them to be acquisitive, dishonest, inauthentic. It implies that the mode of realism itself (once stigmatized as churlish, though distinctly vigorous) is bound up with and so condemned through the illusions and manipulations of the alchemical experiments.

From its context in this group the tale appears to be a last realization of selfish realism so it can be thoroughly and confidently rejected, as the earlier examples of that mode never were, whether they were the class oppositions of Group A or the disturbing social conflicts of the Wife to Pardoner sèquence. It is particularly striking that this rejected model of private greed is also involved in the fantastic creation of gold: Chaucer's historical imagination seems to predict with uncanny accuracy the ground-breaking passage in the *Grundrisse* where Marx describes together money, exchange value and individualism in similarly negative terms.[69]

The Yeoman announces that his Canon is coming, and he sounds very much like the Friar and the Monk together:

> . . . my lord and my soverayn,
> Which that to ryden with yow is ful fayn
> For his desport; he loveth daliaunce.

(590–2)

He also has aspects of the Merchant, according to the language:

> He hath take on hym many a greet emprise,
> Which were ful hard for any that is heere
> To brynge aboute,

(605–7)

Then the vocabulary is reminiscent of that used by the Franklin:

> . . . I dar leye in balaunce
> Al that I have in my possessioun.
> He is a man of heigh discrecioun;

(611–13)

In summary, his powers are remarkable:

> . . . al this ground on which we been ridyng,
> Til that we come to Caunterbury town
> He koude al clene turne it up-so-doun,
> And pave it al of silver and of gold.

> (623–6)

Language and imagery throughout this passage suggest that the Canon is an epitome of the cash-obsessed pilgrims, whether those religious who reverse their role, like Monk, Friar and Pardoner, or more directly mercantile figures from the 'professional' group.

The Canon's Yeoman's tale, that is, so far from being a tale to be rejected as unChaucerian,[70] is a summary of the secular and self-seeking path taken by so many in the tales and the contemporary world, but a summary designed as a transition, constructed so that the whole formation can now be dismissed as a threatening force. The late and hasty arrival, the forcing of the characters on the 'felaweship', the images used of the Canon, the mundane mode of the whole tale itself − all these state the re-focused threat. Then the banal and slipshod nature of the trickery, the self-conscious flight of the Canon, the strong criticism of 'multiplication' at the end − these are the elements of containment which surround the self-seeking mercantile life; the whole cash economy itself is conceived as a fruitless quest for the philosopher's stone, and so it can be dismissed. The Canon's Yeoman's tale is a crucial part of the re-positioning of the whole text in these last tales, enabling the religious conclusion to arise finally and without too much incredibility.

After its potent opening passage, revealing the essence of the Canon and the role of its tale, the text begins its work of steadily filling in details, creating the material world of the actual practices of these manipulative profit-makers, and also providing consistent reminders of their negative value. They live,

> 'In the suburbes of a toun,' quod he,
> 'Lurkynge in hernes and in lanes blynde,
> Whereas thise robbours and thise theves by kynde
> Holden hir pryvee fereful residence,
> As they that dar nat shewen hir presence;
> So faren we, if I shal seye the sothe.'

> (657–62)

The Canon himself is a figure of suspicious and guilty behaviour:

> Whil this Yeman was thus in his talkyng,
> This Chanoun drough hym neer, and herde al thyng
> Which that this Yeman spak, for suspecioun
> Of mennes speche evere hadde this Chanoun.
> For Catoun seith that he that gilty is
> Demeth alle thyng be spoke of hym, ywis.
>
> (684–9)

There follows a confessional prologue where the alchemist's art is projected in detail, but also made negative, as 'This cursed craft' (830), and 'this elvysshe nyce lore' (842). The practices are implicitly condemned by their consistent failure and their diabolic tendency:

> That futur temps hath maad men to dissevere,
> In trust therof, from al that evere they hadde.
> Yet of that art they kan nat wexen sadde,
> For unto hem it is a bitter sweete –
> So semeth it – for nadde they but a sheete,
> Which that they myghte wrappe hem inne anyght,
> And a brat to walken inne by daylyght,
> They wolde hem selle and spenden on this craft.
> They kan nat stynte til no thyng be laft.
> And everemoore, where that evere they goon,
> Men may hem knowe by smel of brymstoon.
>
> (875–85)

The topic of alchemy allows the hellish smell to be naturally developed, but the description itself works just as well for any obsessive investment to make a future profit; the whole world of mercantile practices is gathered in by the ideological imagination and directed towards the everlasting bonfire.

The Yeoman's tale itself has frequently been felt a disappointment.[71] This is because, like most of the tales of the third and last sequence, it merely fills out a purpose already established; it shows the petty manipulation and detailed dishonesty that is basic to those who seek to multiply gold, whether in crucibles or in the privacy of a merchant's accounts office. Detailed and quite droll as it is, the story is simple: it merely gives narrative support to the ideological position already established, building steadily a platform for the ending, where a series of summaries is offered.

First, a socioeconomic one:

> Considereth, sires, how that, in ech estaat,
> Bitwixe men and gold ther is debaat
> So ferforth that unnethes is ther noon.
> This multiplying blent so many oon
> That in good feith I trowe that it bee
> The cause grettest of swich scarsetee.

(1388–93)

Moving on from this practical picture of self-contradiction, the criticism becomes moral and Christian:

> O! fy, for shame! they that han bcen brent
> Allas! kan they nat flee the fires heete?
> Ye that it use, I rede ye it leete,
> Lest ye lese al; for bet than nevere is late.

(1407–10)

The impossibility and impropriety of pursuing the philosophers' stone of profit is stated through authorities, the specifically alchemical Arnold de Villanova and the more generally valid Plato. The story finally turns to an ultimate authority, in both present and future time:

> For unto Crist it is so lief and deere
> That he ne wol nat that it discovered bee,
> But where it liketh to his deitee
> Men for t'enspire, and eek for to dcffende
> Whom that hym liketh; lo, this is the ende.'

(1467–71)

Like Langland, who only found the meaning of 'meed' in its transmutation into undeserved salvation, Chaucer makes divine powers the vanishing point of man's quest for greater secular wealth and power. The image of the philosophers' stone has provided both a potent summary of the greed and self-seeking that was so dramatically and realistically created earlier in the tales, and at the same time the convenient means of ideologically rejecting all those formations of the modern world that the historical imagination of the poet has so powerfully created. The artistic power to realize those forces itself is the topic of the one remaining tale before the Christian resolution of the tales themselves.

The Manciple's tale is one of the least admired in the whole of
The Canterbury Tales; criticism has usually either strained to make
it seem in character with its teller or has confronted its strangely
reductive form in some puzzlement.[72] The position of the tale is
the key to its significance: its insistence on a judicious silence is a
forerunner of the Retractions that follow the Parson's tale.[73]

The headlink is one of the liveliest of all these vignettes of
human conflict. The Host calls on the Cook for a tale, although
he started one long ago in Group A — further evidence of a
change of plan towards the end of the long poem. But he is as
drunk as any churl might be. A Manciple attacks this Cook in
aggressive terms with a malice that, as the Host at once suggests,
may arise from historical conflict over profit between the two
ends of the catering business.

This Manciple back-tracks at once, speaks placatingly to the
Cook and moves to his tale. So his simple moral, that it is wise to
keep your mouth shut, has overtly a mundane and self-seeking
motivation. For commentators who see the *Tales* as no more than
speeches in character, that explains the whole thing: it is just an
urgent defence of an unadmirable worldly shrewdness — say
nothing and no harm can come.

But the modal difference between headlink and tale indicates
that, unlike those of the Miller, Reeve and indeed Cook himself,
this tale is distinctly separate from its teller. It is a formal, indeed
somewhat lifeless piece of developed rhetoric, telling in careful
and unimaginative stages the story of how the crow became
black.[74] The white and fine-voiced crow saw Apollo's wife being
faithless. He told his master and in vengeance was turned black
and deprived of his voice. This brief action is followed by a long
and repetitive statement of the moral: 'keep wel thy tonge'. That,
the speaker says, was taught to him when young:

> My sone, thy tonge sholdestow restreyne
> At alle tymes, but whan thow doost thy peyne
> To speke of God, in honour and preyere.

> (329–31)

It is inevitable, seeing the position of this tale and the whole
development of *The Canterbury Tales*, to read the story and its
moral as having a meaning beyond the reductive motives of this
Manciple. Throughout the early sequences of the *Tales* the poet
himself has reported in detail, sometimes almost gleeful detail,

the real disorderly doings in the world, acts of infidelity both social and familial. Chaucer himself has acted the part of the crow, warning the lords of his world about contemporary threats to their authority.

The image of the fine and entertaining caged bird is not inappropriate for the poet in the aristocratic world. But Chaucer moved from there, in *The Book of Fame* and *The Canterbury Tales* in general, to take in the whole reality of a turbulent society. The journey between *The Book of Fame* and the Retractions is epitomized in the final lines of this strangely potent tale:

> My sone, be war, and be noon auctour newe
> Of tidynges, wheither they been false or trewe.
> Whereso thou come, amonges hye or lowe,
> Kepe wel thy tonge, and thenk upon the crowe.

(359–62)

And yet there remains the fact that this crafty Manciple has his own unpleasantly low and disorderly reasons for telling this tale. It was he who subverted the authority of all the learned men of law who advised all the lords of the land what to do with their property (general prologue, 573–86). And by his presence in the dynamic headlink he must to some degree at least subvert the full conservative ideological containment of the tales themselves. The poet, accepting silence as proper, still reminds the audience of the world he created in the first sections of the poem, through inarticulate Cook and conniving Manciple.

As the Manciple's tale ends, the sun is setting; day and pilgrimage and art are all drawing to an end. The pilgrims are coming to a 'thropes end' (12), moving down the hill from Harbledown. Then suddenly the great Cathedral becomes visible in the declining sun, its Caen stone shining at its lambent, light golden best. Today it is still an imposing sight: in the late fourteenth century, when buildings were lower and religious sensitivities higher, the spectacle would impose massive religious authority. The next tale fulfils and fills out the appropriate mode, the authentic tone of serious, engaged Christianity.

Only one tale is lacking for the 'joly compaignye' (14) to complete their pilgrimage, which has been literary, physical and is now decidely spiritual: the Parson is the right man to 'knytte up wel a greet mateere' (28). He confirms the rejection of mere

literature that has been developing through this last sequence: he
will not 'tellen fables and swich wrecchednesse' (34) and restates
his colleague the Nun's Priest's image of a truly fruitful practice:

> Why shoulde I sowen draf out of my fest,
> Whan I may sowen whete, if that me lest?

> (35–6)

He rejects alliterative poetry (42–3), and 'rym' is 'litel bettre'
(46). So there will follow a 'myrie tale in prose':

> To shewe you the wey, in this viage
> Of thilke parfit glorious pilgrymage
> That highte Jerusalem celestial.

> (49–51)

The sermon that the Parson tells has been viewed by critics either
as a mere pious gesture or as the long-prepared piece of serious
Christianity that Chaucer has always intended. This study has
shown the Parson's tale is an ending which does grow out of the
tales, but not in a simple, predictable or unstrained way.

There are many other analogues from the period for the
Christian position as the final stage of a work which realizes the
problems involved with a simply aristocratic and conservative
view. In *Sir Gawain and the Green Knight* and Malory's Arthuriad,
different sorts of secular dissent and conflict are resolved by the
Christian avowal, though in neither is it a complete or completely
convincing position. It should be clear enough that in a period
when the economic and social forces of the future bourgeois
formation were themselves new, that formation itself had not and
could not be expected to have developed its own cultural self-
consciousness. Consciousness is itself a cultural construct, and a
critique of an existing system does not of itself automatically
produce an alternative place to stand. The Christian position was
a natural, historically inevitable one for someone who could see
the poverty of the feudal and aristocratic viewpoint, could trace
the new world of mercantile and individual values being formed,
but could hardly be expected to conceive of the whole structure of
bourgeois individualism and its complex cultural ideology.

In any case, there were strong new forces within Christianity
itself which were historically dynamic, shaping a newly indivi-
dualized type of religion, whether specifically mystical and so
without institutional structure, or whether inherently revolu-

tionary, as in the Lollard development and its inheritors and analogues throughout Europe. The practices of *devotio moderna*, the consciousness of the dance of death, the affective religious literature itself are all signs that not only was Christianity the one possible location of a standpoint for a non-feudal and dissenting consciousness but that Christianity itself was changing to realize that new position.

In this sense the Parson's tale, as a sermon teaching the individual how to behave acceptably in God's eyes, is itself a historical response, albeit one less dynamic and more cautious than the speculative realizations of new secular patterns that Chaucer had achieved in the earlier parts of the *Tales*. This is confirmed in the mode of the Parson's tale, one of the many hortatory sermons in English, directing the ordinary yet perhaps literate Christian towards a personally decided relation with God. Inherently, 'lay literacy' was a form of *devotio moderna* and had Lollard tendencies;[75] the close connection between Chaucer and the 'Lollard knights' shows it is no accident that he finally speaks in their language, with their seriousness — and also with their social and historical relevance.

The tale itself is taken from a variety of sources and slowly and carefully works its way through the sins and their remedies to achieve, by a full and fully understood penance, a state of grace which is both a promise of future peace and itself a defence against the confusions of the world. The tone is consistently that implied in the description of the Parson in the general prologue, a man speaking plainly to his less well-advised equals, and locating his discourse firmly in each individual's consciousness of the ambient world and the ways in which it may be mastered. The world that has been realized as so turbulent and threatening, to rich and poor alike, from the dissents of the general prologue and the Knight's tale through the whole regime of contrariety, unconvincing repression and self-seeking aggression — this world can only be put to silence, says the Parson, by surrendering to a greater and final authority through this detailed but not complex series of practices.

In many ways the Parson's tale is a religious and non-aristocratic version of the tale of Melibee, providing a cultural, and hopefully real, resolution to the disturbed experience of contemporary life:

Thanne shal men understonde what is the fruyt of penaunce; and, after the word of Jhesu Crist, it is the endelees blisse of hevene, ther joye hath no contrarioustee of wo ne grevaunce; ther alle harmes been passed of this present lyf; ther as is the sikernesse fro the peyne of helle; ther as is the blisful compaignye that rejoysen hem evermo, everich of otheres joye; ther as the body of man, that whilom was foul and derk, is moore cleer than the sonne; ther as the body, that whilom was syk, freele and fieble, and mortal, is inmortal, and so strong and so hool that ther may no thyng apeyren it; ther as ne is neither hunger, thurst, ne coold, but every soule replenyssed with the sighte of the parfit knowynge of God.

(1075–80)

This, says the Parson, and finally *The Canterbury Tales*, is the way to avoid and escape so much of the modern world that the tales have realized. Sickness (the original motive in the general prologue), hunger, thirst and cold, those things that were basic forces in social disorder, the 'contrarioustee' and 'harme' that was a product of the competitive world; here they can all be eluded; here a 'compaignye' will be 'blisful', not noisy and consistently at odds as this pilgrim company has so vividly been.

The Parson's tale does 'quite', match and answer the whole *Canterbury Tales* as Patterson argues,[76] but as with other quitings, through the tales, it does so both in response to the pressure of the real world — which includes religious urges — and as part of a literary edifice that historically realizes the period in all its complexity, secular and religious. The power of the whole enormous effort, the ultimate sign of the teeming vigour of the text is seen in its reflex, the exhaustion of its producer, and this is lastly stated in the Retractions. There, outside the fictional frame story, the 'maker of this book' — no genius author here, simply a cultural producer — takes his leave.

Firmly in the tone of the Parson's sermon, Chaucer speaks regretfully of his 'translacions and enditynges of worldly vanitees,' (1084) and revokes them. Among the revoked works are 'the tales of Caunterbury, thilke that sownen into synne' (1085). Having accepted the Parson's position, he now rejects those tales which realize powerfully the turbulent forces of his own world. The author and his book finally signal their resting place in religion —

enclosed within a historical formation of the period and so no longer analytically realizing the scope and impact of that history. The creation of the whole work however, had such a broad historical power that it still has a place in the continuing history of human productivity and the processes in which it is involved.

A re-reading of *The Canterbury Tales* in the light of modern knowledge about the ways in which texts and their societies interrelate, both in their time and through the succeeding re-creations in other times, has revealed many things. Issues that have puzzled recent humanist critics are often of their own creation, such as the ending of the Pardoner's tale or the role of the Canon's Yeoman's story. Tales that humanist criticism has overlooked have important functions and are much more dynamic than critical blinkers have allowed — the tales of the Physician, the Manciple and Chaucer's own tale of Melibee, for example. And as a whole – to adapt the language of the poem's most stunningly historical and imaginative creation, the Wife of Bath — the long-standing authority of the text rises centrally from its power to create the experience of living in the society and history of the late fourteenth century, an experience which is realized and interpreted throughout this dynamic poem in the most rich and historically imaginative detail.

Abbreviations

CR	Chaucer Review
ELH	English Literary History
ES	Essays and Studies
JEGP	Journal of English and Germanic Philology
YES	Yearbook of English Studies
MAE	Medium Aevum
MP	Modern Philology
RES	Review of English Studies
SAC	Studies of the Age of Chaucer
SP	Studies in Philology
TSE	Tulane Studies in English
UTQ	University of Toronto Quarterly

Notes

Introduction

1 The reputation of Chaucer has been recorded in detailed and sometimes fragmentary form by C. F. E. Spurgeon, *Five Hundred Years of Chaucer Criticism and Allusion* (Cambridge, 1925) and in longer extracts by D. S. Brewer, *Geoffrey Chaucer, The Critical Heritage* series (London, 1978).

2 The political implications of literary criticism have been discussed by R. Ohmann, *English in America* (New York, 1976) and T. Eagleton, 'The Rise of English', chapter 1 of *Literary Theory* (Oxford, 1983). Most of the new critical readings of Chaucer appeared in academic journals such as *Chaucer Review* in its early years but examples in book form are J. L. Speirs, *Chaucer the Maker* (London, 1951) and T. Whittock, *A Reading of the Canterbury Tales* (Cambridge, 1968). The leader of the allegorists is D. W. Robertson, *Preface to Chaucer* (Princeton, 1963).

3 Raymond Williams's *Culture and Society* (London, 1958) and *The Long Revolution* (London, 1961) were opening statements in a critique which has become more explicit and more political, as in *Keywords* (London, 1976) and *Marxism and Literature* (Oxford, 1977). Terry Eagleton's work is also of major weight, especially *Criticism and Ideology* (London, 1976), *Marxism and Literary Criticism* (London, 1976) and *Literary Theory*. Volumes in the 'New Accents' series are often valuable, particularly C. Belsey, *Critical Practice* (London, 1980); T. Bennett, *Formalism and Marxism* (London, 1983); A. Easthope, *Poetry as Discourse* (London, 1983) and P. Widdowson ed., *Re-Reading English* (London, 1982). Other important contributions include F. Jameson, *The Political Unconscious* (London, 1981); P. Macherey, *Theory of Literary Production* (London, 1977) and R. Coward and J. Ellis, *Language and Materialism* (London, 1977).

4   Reference to this work will be made in footnotes to the following chapters, but the following have some methodological importance: S. Delany, *Chaucer's House of Fame: The Poetics of Skeptical Fideism* (Chicago, 1972); D. Aers, *Chaucer, Langland and the Creative Imagination* (London, 1979); P. Strohm, 'Chaucer's Audience', *LH*, 5 (1979), pp. 26–41.

5   Important data beyond the literary texts can be found in books like: W. J. Ong, *Orality and Literacy* (London, 1982); M. J. Clanchy, *From Memory to Written Record* (London, 1979); L. Febvre and H. -J. Martin, *The Coming of the Book* (London, 1976); B. Stock, *The Implications of Literacy* (Princeton, 1983). I have made some attempt in this direction in 'Chaucer and the Sociology of Literature,' *SAC*, 2 (1980), pp. 15–51 and 'Textual Variants: Textual Variance', *Southern Review* 16 (Adelaide), (1983), pp. 44–54.

6   See *The Works of Geoffrey Chaucer*, ed. F. N. Robinson, 2nd edn. (Cambridge, 1957), p. 787.

7   *The Paston Letters*, ed. N. C. Davis (Oxford, 1971); *The Anonimalle Chronicle*, ed. V. H. Galbraith (Manchester, 1970); M. McKisack, *The Fourteenth Century* (Oxford, 1959); J. L. Bolton, *The Medieval English Economy* (London, 1980); J. Hatcher, *Plague, Population and the English Economy* (London, 1977); J. Gardner, *The Life and Times of Geoffrey Chaucer* (London, 1977); J. Armitage-Smith, *John of Gaunt* (London, 1904).

Chapter 1   Dream Poems and Chaucer's World

1   C. Erickson, *The Medieval Vision* (New York, 1976), chapters 1 and 2, and A. C. Spearing, *Medieval Dream Poetry* (Cambridge, 1976), chapter 1.

2   M. M. Crow and C. C. Olson, *Chaucer Life-Records* (Oxford, 1966).

3   D. W. Robertson, 'The Historical Setting of Chaucer's *Book of the Duchess*', in *Essays in Medieval Culture* (Princeton, 1980), p. 237.

4   For the date of Blanche's death, see J. N. Palmer, 'The Historical Content of *The Book of the Duchess*', *CR*, 8 (1974), pp. 253–6. For 'in youthe', see the Man of Law's prologue, line 57; quotations are taken from F. N. Robinson ed., *The Works of Geoffrey Chaucer*, 2nd edn. (Boston, 1957).

5   Crow and Olson, *Chaucer Life-Records*, p. 271.

6   On Gothic form, see C. Muscatine, *Chaucer and the French Tradition* (Berkeley, 1957), pp. 167–73; R. M. Jordan, *Chaucer and the Shape of Creation* (New Haven, 1967), chapters 1–3.

7   For a survey, see Robinson, *The Works of Geoffrey Chaucer*, p. 773.

8   R. M. Jordan, 'The Compositional Structure of the *Book of the*

Duchess', *CR*, 9 (1974), pp. 99–117, and Spearing, *Medieval Dream Poetry*, pp. 66–71.

9   W. Clemen, *Chaucer's Early Poetry* (London, 1963), pp. 31–6.

10 M. Lambert, *Style and Vision in Malory's More Darthur* (New Haven, 1975), pp. 176–94.

11 For an influential statement of this position, see J. Lawlor, 'The Pattern of Consolation in *The Book of the Duchess'*, *Speculum*, 31 (1950), pp. 626–48; reprinted in *Chaucer Criticism*, vol. 2, ed. R. J. Schoeck and J. Taylor (Notre Dame, 1960).

12 The phrase is from M. James, *English Politics and the Concept of Honour* (Oxford, 1979), p. 1; for a discussion of the matter, see S. Knight, *Arthurian Literature and Society* (London, 1983), pp. 116–17.

13 G. Duby, 'Youth in Aristocratic Society', in *The Chivalrous Society* (London, 1977).

14 J. A. W. Bennett, *Chaucer's Book of Fame* (Oxford, 1968), p. ix.

15 Crow and Olson, *Chaucer Life-Records*, p. 173.

16 Crow and Olson, *Chaucer Life-Records*, pp. 152–7.

17 Crow and Olson, *Chaucer Life-Records*, pp. 32–40.

18 S. Delany, *Chaucer's House of Fame: The Poetics of Skeptical Fideism* (Chicago, 1972), p. 16.

19 Muscatine, *Chaucer and the French Tradition*, pp. 107–15.

20 Delany, chapters 2 and 3.

21 For the eagle and Dante, see Bennett, *Chaucer's Book of Fame*, pp. 49–51; for it as Christian allegory, see B. G. Koonce, *Chaucer and the Tradition of Fame* (Princeton, 1966), pp. 143–77.

22 Bennett, *Chaucer's Book of Fame*, chapter 2.

23 Bennett, *Chaucer's Book of Fame*, pp. 122–4.

24 D. A. Pearsall, 'The *Troilus* Frontispiece and Chaucer's Audience', *YES*, 7 (1977), pp. 68–74; P. Strohm, 'Chaucer's Audience', *LH*, 5 (1977), pp. 26–41; A. Middleton, 'Chaucer's New Men and the Good of Literature in *The Canterbury Tales'*, in E. Said ed., *Literature and Society* (Baltimore, 1980).

25 D. A. Pearsall, *Old and Middle English Poetry* (London, 1976), pp. 194–7.

26 Sir John Clanvowe, *The Works*, ed. V. J. Scattergood (Ipswich, 1975).

27 E. Auerbach, 'Sermo Humilis' in *Literary Language and Its Public in Late Latin Antiquity and in the Middle Ages* (London, 1965).

28 B. K. Cowgill, '*The Parlement of Foules* and the Body Politic', *JEGP*, 74 (1975), pp. 313–35.

29 Bennett, *The Parlement of Foules* (Oxford, 1957), pp. 31–46.

30 Robinson discusses the possibilities, *The Works of Geoffrey Chaucer*, p. 793, note on line 117.

31 D. Aers, '*The Parliament of Fowls*: Authority, the Knower and the Known', *CR*, 16 (1981), pp. 1–17, see pp. 8–9.

32   Bennett, *The Parlement of Foules*, chapters 3 and 4.
33   D. S. Brewer ed., *The Parlement of Foulys* (London, 1960), p. 20; Bennett, *The Parlement of Foules*, p. 91.
34   Bennett, *The Parlement of Foules*, chapter 3.
35   Brewer, *The Parlement of Foulys*, pp. 3–13.
36   F. Thompson, *A Short History of Parliament 1295–1642* (Minneapolis, 1953).
37   K. Malone, *Chapters on Chaucer* (Cambridge, Mass., 1951), pp. 71–2; Bennett, *The Parlement of Foules*, pp. 166–9; Brewer, *The Parlement of Fowlys*, pp. 37–8.
38   E. Rickert, 'A New Interpretation of *The Parlement of Foules*', *MP*, 18 (1920), pp. 1–29; J. Gardner, *The Life and Times of Chaucer* (London, 1977), pp. 218–21.
39   D. Chamberlain, 'The Music of the Spheres and *The Parlement of Foules*', *CR*, 5 (1970), pp. 32–56.

Chapter 2   *Troilus and Criseyde*

1   See respectively G. L. Kittredge, *Chaucer's Poetry* (Cambridge, Mass., 1915), pp. 117–21 and J. P. McCall, 'The Trojan Scene in Chaucer's *Troilus*', *ELH*, 29 (1962), pp. 263–75.
2   See M. Sundwall, '*The Destruction of Troy*, Chaucer's *Troilus and Criseyde* and Lydgate's *Troy Book*', *RES*, 26 (1925), pp. 313–17; J. P. McCall and G. Rudisill, 'The Parliament of 1386 and Chaucer's Trojan Parliament', *JEGP*, 58 (1959), pp. 276–88; D. W. Robertson, 'The Concept of Courtly Love as an Impediment to the Understanding of Medieval Texts', in *Essays in Medieval Culture* (Princeton, 1980), pp. 265–72.
3   C. D. Benson, *The History of Troy in Middle English Literature* (Woodbridge, 1980), pp. 135–6; L. W. Patterson, 'Ambiguity and Interpretation: A Fifteenth Century Reading of *Troilus and Criseyde*', *Speculum*, 54 (1979), pp. 297–330, see p. 324; H. M. Smyser, 'The Domestic Background of *Troilus and Criseyde*', *Speculum*, 31 (1956), pp. 297–315; M. W. Bloomfield, 'Chaucer's Sense of History', *JEGP*, 51 (1952), pp. 301–13.
4   D. Aers, 'Chaucer's Criseyde: Woman in Society: Woman in Love', in *Chaucer, Langland and the Creative Imagination* (London, 1980), chapter 5; this is a slightly altered version of the essay published in *CR*, 13 (1979), pp. 177–200.
5   F. N. Robinson, ed., *The Works of Geoffrey Chaucer*, 2nd edn. (Boston, 1957), pp. 810–11.
6   A. C. Spearing, *Troilus and Criseyde* (London, 1976), pp. 33–5.
7   C. Muscatine, *Chaucer and the French Tradition* (Berkeley, 1957); J. A. Burrow, *Ricardian Poetry* (London, 1972).

8   M. James, *English Politics and the Concept of Honour* (Oxford, 1979).

9   R. W. Hanning, *The Individual and Society in Twelfth Century Romance* (New Haven, 1972); P. Dronke, *Poetic Individualism in the Middle Ages* (Oxford, 1970); C. Morris, *The Discovery of the Individual* (London, 1972); A. Macfarlane, *The Origins of English Individualism* (Oxford, 1978); R. W. Southern, *The Making of the Middle Ages* (London, 1953).

10 P. L. Berger and T. Luckmann, *The Social Construction of Reality* (London, 1971).

11 For the fuller discussion of these patterns, see S. Knight, *Arthurian Literature and Society* (London, 1983), chapter 3.

12 M. Fries, ' "Slydynge of Corage": Chaucer's Criseyde as Feminist Victim', in A. Diamond and L. R. Edwards, eds., *The Authority of Experience* (Amherst, 1977), pp. 45–59.

13 D. W. Rowe, *'O Love! O Charite!': Contraries Harmonized in Chaucer's Troilus* (Carbondale, 1976).

14 See respectively E. Salter, '*Troilus and Criseyde*: a Reconsideration', in J. Lawlor ed. *Essays in Memory of C. S. Lewis* (London, 1966), pp. 86–106 and J. L. Shanley, 'The *Troilus* and Christian Love', *ELH*, 6 (1939), pp. 271–81, reprinted in R. J. Schoeck and J. Taylor eds., *Chaucer Criticism*, vol. 2 (Notre Dame, 1960) and in E. Wagenknecht ed., *Chaucer: Modern Essays in Criticism* (New York, 1959).

15 D. C. Boughner, 'Elements of Epic Grandeur in the *Troilus*', *ELH*, 6 (1939), pp. 200–10, reprinted in *Chaucer Criticism*, vol. 2, and H. L. Rogers, 'The Beginning (and Ending) of Chaucer's *Troilus and Criseyde*', in A. Stephens, H. L. Rogers and B. Coghlan eds., *Festschrift for Ralph Farrell* (Bern, 1977).

16 R. M. Jordan, *Chaucer and the Shape of Creation* (Cambridge, Mass., 1967), see chapter 4.

17 On this topic see D. W. Robertson, *Preface to Chaucer* (Princeton, 1963), chapters 1 and 2 and Muscatine, *Chaucer and the French Tradition*, pp. 167–72.

18 Spearing, *Troilus and Criseyde*, p. 17.

19 I. Bishop, *Chaucer's Troilus and Criseyde* (Bristol, 1981), p. 47.

20 For a discussion, see S. A. Meech, *Design in Chaucer's Troilus* (New York, 1959), pp. 12–19.

21 Muscatine, *Chaucer and the French Tradition*, chapter 5.

22 M. A. K. Halliday, *Language as a Social Semiotic* (London, 1974).

23 M. McAlpine, *The Genre of Troilus and Criseyde* (Ithaca, 1978).

24 C. S. Lewis, 'What Chaucer Really Did to *Il Filostrato*', *ES*, 17 (1932), pp. 56–75, reprinted in *Chaucer Criticism*, vol. 2.

25 B. A. Windeatt, 'Introduction' to *Troilus and Criseyde* (London, 1984), p. 10.

26 The illustration is discussed by D. A. Pearsall, 'The *Troilus* Frontispiece and Chaucer's Audience', *YES*, 7 (1977), pp. 68–74;

the 'imagined audience' is proposed by D. Mehl, 'Chaucer's Audience', *Leeds Studies in English*, 10 (1976), pp. 1–12. A symposium on Chaucer's audience appears in *CR*, 18 (1983), pp. 137–81, and the notion of a dual audience, one real and one implied, is recurrent through the papers and discussion.

27　Lewis, 'What Chaucer Really Did to *Il Filostrato*'; Windeatt, *Troilus and Criseyde*, p. 9.

28　R. M. Lumiansky, 'The Function of the Proverbial Monitory Elements in Chaucer's *Troilus and Criseyde*', *TSE*, 2 (1950), pp. 5–48.

29　G. Mieskowski, 'The Reputation of Criseyde', *Transactions of the Connecticut Academy of Arts and Science*, 43 (1971), pp. 71–153, see p. 99; reprinted as a monograph (Hampden, 1971).

30　M. Lambert, 'Troilus, Book 1–III: A Criseydan Reading', *Essays on Troilus and Criseyde*, ed. M. Salu (Cambridge, 1979), pp. 105–25; Bishop, *Chaucer's Troilus and Criseyde*, p. 19; Muscatine, *Chaucer and the French Tradition*, pp. 153–41.

31　M. Fries, ' "Slydynge of Corage": Chaucer's Criseyde as Feminist Victim'; Aers, 'Chaucer's Criseyde: Woman in Society: Woman in Love'; Delany, 'The Technique of Alienation in *Troilus and Criseyde*', in A. P. Foulkes, ed., *The Uses of Criticism* (Frankfurt, 1976), pp. 77–95, see pp. 77–78; A. Diamond, 'Chaucer's Women and Women's Chaucer', in *The Authority of Experience*, pp. 66–88, see p. 87.

32　S. Knight, *Rymyng Craftily: Meaning in Chaucer's Poetry* (Sydney, 1973), pp. 50–6.

33　Aers, 'Chaucer's Criseyde: Woman in Society: Woman in Love", p. 14.

34　Bishop, *Chaucer's Troilus and Criseyde*, p. 32.

35　R. E. Kaske, 'The Aube in Chaucer's Troilus', in *Chaucer Criticism*, vol. 2.

36　Aers, 'Chaucer's Criseyde: Woman in Society: Woman in Love', p. 129.

37　McCall and Rudisill, 'The Parliament of 1386 and Chaucer's Trojan Parliament'.

38　D. Anderson, 'Theban History in Chaucer's Troilus', *SAC*, 4 (1982), pp. 109–33.

39　Windeatt, *Troilus and Criseyde*, pp. 19–24.

40　D. W. Robertson, 'Chaucerian Tragedy', *ELH*, 19 (1952), pp. 1–37, see p. 26, reprinted in *Chaucer Criticism*, vol. 2.

41　A. Lockhart, 'Semantic, Moral and Aesthetic Degeneration in *Troilus and Criseyde*', *CR*, 8 (1973), pp. 100–18.

42　I. L. Gordon, *The Double Sorrow of Troilus: A Study of Ambiguities in Troilus and Criseyde* (Oxford, 1970), see p. 132.

43　E. T. Donaldson, 'Criseyde and her Narrator', in *Speaking of Chaucer* (London, 1970), pp. 65–83.

44　W. C. Curry, 'Destiny in *Troilus and Criseyde*', in *Chaucer and the*

Medieval Sciences, 2nd edn. (London, 1960), chapter 10, reprinted in *Chaucer Criticism*, vol. 2; Aers, 'Chaucer's Criseyde: Woman in Society: Woman in Love', pp. 139–41.

45 R. W. Frank, *Chaucer and the Legend of Good Women* (Cambridge, Mass., 1972), see pp. 88–90 and 131.

46 G. Williams, *A New View of Chaucer* (Durham, N. Carolina, 1965).

Chapter 3 *The Canterbury Tales*

1 E. T. Donaldson, 'The Manuscripts of Chaucer's Work and Their Use', in *Geoffrey Chaucer*, (ed.) D. S. Brewer (London, 1974).

2 For a full discussion of the concept see R. Williams, *Politics and Letters* (London, 1979), pp. 156–74.

3 S. Delany, 'Womanliness in the Man of Law's Tale', *CR*, 9 (1974), pp. 63–72, see p. 70; D. R. Pichaske and L. Swetland, 'Chaucer and the Medieval Monarchy: Harry Bailly in the *Canterbury Tales*', *CR*, 11 (1977), pp. 179–200, see pp. 185–6; D. W. Robertson, 'Chaucer and the "Commune Profit": the Manor', *Medievalia*, 6 (1980), pp. 229–59, see p. 232.

4 C. R. Oman, *The Great Revolt* (Oxford, 1906), p. 40.

5 For Chaucer's wardships, see M. M. Crow and C. C. Olson, *Chaucer Life-Records* (Oxford, 1966), pp. 294–302; for Sturry, see K. B. McFarlane, *Lancastrian Kings and Lollard Knights* (Oxford, 1972), p. 163.

6 For the story of Joan of Kent, see R. B. Dobson ed., *The Peasants' Revolt of 1381*, 2nd edn. (London, 1983), pp. 133 and 139; J. Froissart, *Chronicles* (London, 1968), pp. 229–30.

7 My own editorial work confirms the approach taken by L. D. Benson in 'The Order of The Canterbury Tales', *SAC*, 3 (1982), pp. 71–120.

8 H. F. Brooks, *Chaucer's Pilgrims* (London, 1962), see p. 1.

9 Recent and clear examples of this argument are in D. S. Brewer, 'Class and Class Distinction in Chaucer', in *Tradition and Innovation in Chaucer* (London, 1982), pp. 54–5 and F. R. H. Du Boulay, 'The Historical Chaucer', in *Geoffrey Chaucer*, ed. D. S. Brewer (London, 1974), see note 2, pp. 36–7.

10 J. Mann, *Chaucer and Medieval Estates Satire* (Cambridge, 1973), see p. 6.

11 D. R. Howard, *The Idea of The Canterbury Tales* (Berkeley, 1976), p. 113.

12 K. Marx, *Grundrisse* (London, 1973), p. 512.

13 D. W. Robertson, ' "And for my land thus hastow mordred me": Land Tenure, the Cloth Industry and the Wife of Bath', *CR*, 14 (1980), pp. 403–20.

14 J. Hatcher, *Plague, Population and the English Economy 1348–1530* (London, 1977).

15 S. Knight, *Arthurian Literature and Society* (London, 1983), chapter 3.

16 T. Jones, *Chaucer's Knight: The Portrait of a Mercenary* (London, 1980).

17 A survey of the topic is given by R. Boase, *The Origin and Meaning of Courtly Love* (Manchester, 1977).

18 G. Duby, 'Youth in Aristocratic Society', in *The Chivalrous Society* (London, 1977) and Knight, *Arthurian Literature and Society*, chapter 3.

19 H. Specht, *Chaucer's Franklin and Canterbury Tales* (Copenhagen, 1981); N. Saul, 'The Social Status of Chaucer's Franklin: A Reconsideration', *MÆ*, 52 (1983), pp. 10–26.

20 Mann, *Chaucer and Medieval Estates Satire*, chapter 4.

21 Robertson, 'Land Tenure, the Cloth Industry and the Wife of Bath'.

22 G. Stilwell, 'Chaucer's Plowman and the Contemporary English Peasant', *ELH*, 6 (1939), pp. 285–90, see p. 285.

23 See K. Sisam ed., *Fourteenth Century Verse and Prose* (Oxford, 1955), pp. 160–1 and for similar letters *Chronicon Henrici Knighton*, ed. J. R. Lumby (Rolls Series, 1895), ii, p. 139.

24 For the status of millers, see M. Bowden, *A Commentary on the General Prologue to The Canterbury Tales* (New York, 1948), p. 24, and for millers in 1381 see R. H. Hilton, *Bond Men Made Free* (London, 1973), pp. 176–9.

25 Brewer, 'Class Distinction in Chaucer', p. 70.

26 C. Muscatine, *Chaucer and the French Tradition* (Berkeley, 1957), pp. 189–90.

27 A. C. Spearing ed., *The Knight's Tale* (Cambridge, 1966), p. 78; E. Salter, *The Knight's Tale and the Clerk's Tale* (London, 1962), pp. 31–2; P. Neuse, 'The Knight: The First Mover in Chaucer's Human Comedy', *UTQ*, 31 (1962), pp. 294–315, reprinted in *Geoffrey Chaucer*, ed. J. A. Burrow (London, 1969), see p. 243.

28 S. Knight, 'The Social Function of the Middle English Romances', in D. Aers (ed.) *Re-Reading Medieval Literature* (Brighton, 1986).

29 H. E. Weissmann, 'Antifeminism and Chaucer's Characterization of Women', in *Geoffrey Chaucer*, ed. G. Economou (New York, 1975), pp. 97–8.

30 Duby, 'Youth in Aristocratic Society', pp. 120–2.

31 M. James, *English Politics and the Concept of Honour* (London, 1979), p. 1 and D. Aers, *Chaucer, Langland and the Creative Imagination* (London, 1980), pp. 176–7.

32 A. C. Spearing, *The Knight's Tale*, p. 78; see also Aers, *Chaucer, Langland and the Creative Imagination*, p. 187.

33 L. W. Patterson, ' "For the Wyves Love of Bathe": Feminine Rhetoric and Poetic Resolution in the *Roman de la Rose* and *The Canterbury Tales*', *Speculum*, 58 (1983), pp. 656–95.

34 B. K. Martin, 'The Miller's Tale as Critical Problem and Dirty Joke', in *Studies in Chaucer* (Sydney, 1982); J. A. W. Bennett, *Chaucer at Oxford and Cambridge* (Oxford, 1974).

35 Muscatine, *Chaucer and the French Tradition*, pp. 225–6.

36 Muscatine, *Chaucer and the French Tradition*, pp. 69–72; Jordan, *Chaucer and the Shape of Creation*, chapters 2, 3 and 7.

37 Weissemann, 'Antifeminism and Chaucer's Characterization of Women', p. 103.

38 M. Aston, 'Lollards and Sedition: 1381–1431', in *Peasants, Knights and Heretics*, ed. R. H. Hilton (Cambridge, 1968).

39 The same point about the relationship of the Man of Law's tale with the preceeding material is made by V. A. Kolve in his recent book *Chaucer and the Imagery of Narrative* (London, 1984).

40 Delany, 'Womanliness in the Man of Law's Tale', p. 70.

41 Delany, 'Womanliness in the Man of Law's Tale', p. 63.

42 M. Schlauch, *Chaucer's Constance and Accused Queens* (New York, 1927).

43 Robertson, 'Land Tenure, The Cloth Industry and the Wife of Bath'. See also Sheila Delany, 'Sexual Economics, Chaucer's Wife of Bath and *The Book of Margery Kempe*', *Minnesota Review*, NS, 5 (1975), pp. 104–15.

44 Robertson, 'Land Tenure, the Cloth Industry and the Wife of Bath', p. 415.

45 Aston, see note 38.

46 Robertson, 'Land Tenure, the Cloth Industry and the Wife of Bath'; A. S. Haskell, 'The Paston Women on Marriage in Fifteenth Century England', *Viator*, 4 (1973), pp. 459–71.

47 Knight, 'The Social Function of the Middle English Romance'.

48 Brewer, 'Class Distinction in Chaucer', pp. 67–8.

49 T. Hahn and R. W. Kaeuper, 'Text and Context: Chaucer's Friar's Tale', *SAC*, 5 (1982), pp. 67–101.

50 K. Marx, *Grundrisse*, pp. 156–8.

51 G. L. Kittredge, *Chaucer and His Poetry* (Boston, 1915), chapter 6.

52 L. D. Benson, 'The Order of *The Canterbury Tales*'.

53 Aers, *Chaucer, Langland and the Creative Imagination*, p. 172.

54 M. Bakhtin, *Rabelais and His World* (Cambridge, Mass., 1968).

55 Marx, *Grundrisse*, pp. 156–8, *Capital*, vol. I (London, 1976), pp. 161–72.

56 Aers, *Chaucer, Langland and the Creative Imagination*, p. 152. The mercantile character of the tale has been raised in different ways by P. A. Olson, 'Chaucer's Merchant and January's "Hevene in Erthe Heere" ', *ELH*, 28 (1961), pp. 203–14 and M. Schlauch, 'Chaucer's Merchant's Tale and Courtly Love', ELH, 4 (1937), pp. 201–12.

57 S. Knight, 'Ideology in the *Franklin's Tale*', *Parergon*, 28 (1980), pp.

3–35; R. Bromwich, 'Celtic Dynastic Themes and the Breton Lays', *Etudes Celtiques*, 9 (1961), pp. 439–74.

58 S. Delany, 'Politics and the Paralysis of Poetic Imagination in *The Physician's Tale*', *SAC*, 3 (1981), pp. 47–60.

59 W. Scheps, 'Chaucer's Numismatic Pardoner and the Personification of Avarice', *Acta*, 4 (1977), pp. 107–23; see pp. 110–11.

60 For 'carrying trade,' see Marx, *Capital*, I, pp. 320–6; for the pool of profit, see *Capital*, I, pp. 130–1 and 588; for primitive manufacturing, see *Grundrisse*, p. 510; for urban feudalism, see *Grundrisse*, p. 512.

61 Hatcher, *Plague, Population and the English Economy*.

62 Marx, *Capital*, I, pp. 163–77.

63 R. J. Schoeck, 'Chaucer's Prioress: Mercy and Tender Heart', in *Chaucer Criticism*, vol. 1, ed. R. J. Schoeck and J. Taylor (Notre Dame, 1960); F, Ridley, *The Prioress and the Critics* (Berkeley, 1965).

64 G. H. Russell, 'Chaucer: The Prioress's Tale', in *Medieval Literature and Civilization*, ed. D. A. Pearsall and R. W. Waldron (London, 1969); J. R. Hirsh, 'Reopening the Prioress's Tale', *CR*, 10 (1975), pp. 30–45.

65 A. B. Friedman, 'The Prioress's Tale and Chaucer's Anti-Semitism', *CR*, 9 (1974), pp. 118–29.

66 J. A. Burrow, 'Four Notes on Sir Thopas', in *Essays on Medieval Literature* (Oxford, 1984).

67 Gardner, *The Life and Times of Chaucer*, p. 288.

68 G. Stilwell, 'The Political Meaning of Chaucer's tale of Melibee', *Speculum*, 9 (1944), pp. 433–46; J. L. Hotson, 'The Tale of Melibeus and John of Gaunt', *SP*, 18 (1921), pp. 429–52; Howard, *The Idea of The Canterbury Tales*, p. 315; W. W. Lawrence, 'Chaucer's Tale of Melibeus', in *Essays and Studies in Honor of Carleton Brown* (New York, 1940), see p. 109; Aers, *Chaucer, Langland and the Creative Imagination*, p. 229.

69 Marx, *Grundrisse*, pp. 156–8.

70 N. F. Blake, Introduction to *The Canterbury Tales* (London, 1980).

71 P. Brown, 'Is the Canon's Yeoman's Tale Apocryphal?' *English Studies*, 64 (1983), pp. 481–90.

72 For a survey see D. C. Baker's 'Critical Commentary' in *The Manciple's Tale* (Norman, 1983).

73 Howard, *The Idea of The Canterbury Tales*, pp. 303–4.

74 S. Knight, *Rymyng Craftily: Meaning in Chaucer's Poetry* (Sydney, 1973), chapter 5.

75 McFarlane, *Lancastrian Kings and Lollard Knights*, p. 225.

76 L. W. Patterson, 'The Parson's Tale and the Setting of The Canterbury Tales', *Traditio*, 34 (1978), pp. 331–80.

Index